Praise for *The Future of Time*

There are so many ways in which we talk about time, think about time and worry about time. But how many of us as leaders really put the necessary time into managing time? *The Future of Time* is a must-read for anyone who, like me, works in a knowledge and ideas business where time and people are your two most valuable assets. It will save many hours, in many days, for you and many others.

Lord Carter, Stephen A. Carter CBE, Group Chief Executive, Informa plc

Every leader who is interested in building an inclusive culture, maximizing the benefits of highly engaged and empowered people and nurturing innovation, productivity and profitability should read this book. Time is the invisible frontier that must be embraced and put at the heart of all organizations that wish to thrive and build sustainably towards a better future for all. Helen captures the potential time offers for intelligent growth and how to bring it to life in your organization.

Caroline Waters OBE

The Future of Time is a practical and well-written antidote to the dehumanization of the modern workplace. Helen inspires us not to *serve* time or to *pass* it, but to be courageous in changing how we see it. By doing this, we can create the opportunity for deeper meaning in our work, for richer connections with our co-workers and for greater value to our organizations.

Simon McBride, Head of People & Organization, Investec plc

The COVID-19 pandemic has triggered a re-evaluation of the workplace and the way we work. *The Future of Time* is highly relevant: it challenges us to reassess our attitude towards time at work from many different perspectives, and to create a time-aware culture fit for purpose in today's world. Solutions that enable the effective use of time and time intelligent leadership are examined. The result is a thought-provoking and invaluable guide to the role of time in the future of work, which will benefit employers and employees alike.

Dame Janet Gaymer DBE, QC (Hon.)

Helen has a way of writing that is captivating and thought-provoking. *The Future of Time* makes us think of time in a new, more 'twenty-first century' way. As people increasingly work from home, the frameworks that Helen offers will make a real, practical difference in the workplace.

Dr Julie Humphreys, Group Head of Diversity and Inclusion, Reach plc

Our time is precious. As someone who tries to fit too much of everything in, this book made me think as a worker, a chief exec, a husband and a human. Helen presents a compelling picture of why we need to think about time differently and offers practical, clear strategies for change.

Simon Blake OBE

I loved this book. It reflects Helen's style: calm, inclusive, reflective and with a laser-sharp focus on solutions to the problem. The format made my heart sing: a clear description of the issue, well referenced, with excellent summaries at the end of each chapter.

The Future of Time could make such a difference to the world of work for so many people. It tackles head on the BIG question that businesses should be answering for themselves: What is the impact to society as a whole, to increasing levels of inequality, and to business profitability and productivity, when knowledge workers are 'subsidizing' their paid hours with unpaid hours? The way we view time is broken. Helen has the solution.

Jane van Zyl, Chief Executive, Working Families

Forget piecemeal wellbeing solutions. If you're a leader looking for a wellbeing strategy that works, then I urge you to read *The Future of Time*. Absorbing and insightful, it explains how businesses and individuals are suffering from the dual tyranny of overwork and wasted working time. Helen sets out a compelling blueprint for how businesses can achieve high levels of performance and employee wellbeing, however fast-paced and demanding your industry.

Neil Laybourn, mental health campaigner, keynote speaker and founder of the 'This Can Happen' conference

If you are looking to create systematic change within your organization, look no further than *The Future of Time*. In this insightful and action-packed book, Helen Beedham gives leaders the tools to identify common time deficits, overcome collective time-blindness, and put in place tactical steps to re-work time, improve engagement and bolster productivity. With employees more exhausted than ever, and organizations losing their best talent to time poverty, this book comes at a perfect moment. Now is the time for leaders to act, and Helen provides everything leaders need to take the first steps toward collective time affluence.

Ashley Whillans, Assistant Professor of Business Administration, Harvard Business School and author of Time Smart

The
Future
of
Time

How 're-working' time can help you boost productivity, diversity and wellbeing

HELEN BEEDHAM

First published in Great Britain by Practical Inspiration Publishing, 2022

© Helen Beedham, 2022

The moral rights of the author have been asserted

ISBN   9781788602631 (print)
        9781788602624 (epub)
        9781788602617 (mobi)

For John

Contents

Introduction

'If you knew Time as well as I do,' said the Hatter, *'you wouldn't talk about wasting it. It's him.' 'I don't know what you mean,'* said Alice. *'Of course you don't!'* the Hatter said, tossing his head contemptuously. *'I dare say you never even spoke to Time!'*

Lewis Carroll, *Alice's Adventures in Wonderland*

Our relationship with time

CLOCKING IN AND out. Filling in timesheets. Working 60- to 70-hour weeks. Pulling all-nighters. Working part-time roles with full-time workloads. Enjoying some time freedom. Bemoaning time poverty. Battling blurry boundaries. Making the most of fragmented time as a working parent. Always chasing the urgent. Often postponing the important. Needing to put in more time to be recognized as committed. Snatching snippets of leftover time for me.

These are my experiences of working time during my professional career. Your experiences undoubtedly will be different, shaped by your own age, identity, personality, career choices and home life. However, over the years I've conducted countless pieces of organizational research and digested thousands of employees' responses to a wide range of questions about their work lives and the organizations in which they work. I've found that some common themes always recur. What I hear is this:

Most people in professional organizations want to work, and broadly enjoy what they do. They value the social connections and sense of purpose they gain from their jobs. They are proud of being able to support others financially and materially. In these difficult economic times, they are relieved simply to have a job that pays the bills and hopefully a bit more.

But many are constantly frustrated by the ever-increasing demands on their working time and the lack of freedom to get on and deliver the important stuff. They get sucked into endless meetings. They have email inboxes that fill up faster than they can empty them. They have to deliver an ever-increasing set of responsibilities, many of which are on top of the 'core job' they were originally hired to do. They have little control over their own time until they get to the most senior levels – if then. In many organizations, they aren't trusted to do a good job or selected for opportunities if they aren't spending time physically in the office. People are exhausted from working relentlessly long hours and, in many cases, juggling additional commitments outside of work. They aren't as fit or healthy as they'd like to be because time to rest, eat healthily and exercise ends up being squeezed into tiny shreds left over when work is finally 'done' for the day. Some have to work harder and longer in order to access the same opportunities afforded to their colleagues. Often people aren't able to progress in their jobs and careers as much or as fast as they'd like to, either because the additional sacrifices they'd have to make are too great or because their background or circumstances disadvantage them in some way.

The more I pondered these experiences, the more I realized that at the heart of them lies our problematic attitude towards time at work. There are some big questions we're not facing up to.

Time is our most valuable asset

Business owners and executives tend to talk about their people being their most valuable asset, which is right and good. But I suggest there is another way of framing this: *time* is the most valuable asset. I should add here that, broadly speaking, this book refers mainly to businesses that provide intangible products and services rather than those industries that require raw materials, plant and machinery to manufacture or distribute tangible goods. However, some of the principles will still apply across different types of business, regardless of what industry you're in.

Our time is finite: no one gets more than 24 hours in a day. So what we all do with our time becomes the most important question. What value do we place on our time? How do we use our time at work? What choices and tradeoffs do we make? What impact do these have?

These are big questions. But they aren't questions to which we pay much attention; in fact, we mostly ignore them. I don't recall talking with colleagues or managers over the years about what we collectively spent our hours on and whether we were making the right choices. I've rarely heard business leaders talk about their own use of time – what they invested their time in and what they chose not to invest time in – or seen them take steps to free up our time so we can focus on the work that really matters.

Instead, we carry on much as we've always done. Our collective attitudes and habits with regard to time at work remain largely fixed, year after year. We are stuck in an old way of operating that isn't beneficial to our health, our productivity or our businesses.

Our time culture at work is broken

Most people have heard about an organization's culture; some find it an intangible concept to get their heads around. A good definition of culture on which I rely is Edgar Schein's definition:[1]

shared, basic assumptions held by members of a group or organization, developed from shared learning experiences. CEOs, organizational experts and management gurus all recognize that to perform highly, enjoy competitive advantage and sustain growth over the longer term, businesses need to have a strong, healthy culture.

So what is our time culture? If organizational culture in general consists of shared assumptions, then time culture specifically is our collective attitudes, values and behaviours at work in relation to time. It covers how we think about time, how we value it and how we live those beliefs through our day-to-day actions, words and decisions. Time culture impacts and informs the usually unspoken assumptions, norms and behaviours about working hours, being available to participate in meetings and conversations, being responsive to requests, meeting deadlines over which you may not have any influence. In the Western corporate world, our time culture typically is characterized by short-termism, speed and volume: fitting a huge amount of effort and activity into a working day or week, multitasking, responding immediately to questions or requests, and paying close attention to daily, weekly, monthly or quarterly results. Our time culture is also characterized by bureaucracy – the plethora of processes, structures, organizational layers and governance protocols that we create and that shape the way we work.

This time culture is deeply ingrained. It's so embedded in the way our organizations are designed, in our business 'norms' and in our historical approach to working that we rarely stop to think about it or question it. It is only when it causes us or our businesses extreme pain that we are jolted into a realization that we need to 'fix' things.

This time culture is hurting us as individuals. There are winners and losers; the winners are those employees whose home lives or backgrounds enable them to 'fit in' and who can 'give what it takes' to get ahead by accepting without question this unspoken deal regarding time. Other employees, who for a whole variety of reasons would benefit from a different deal, see their jobs become unsustainable and their careers progress more slowly or stagnate. This really bothers me. I believe in equality in the workplace: getting into a professional organization and flourishing there should be a possibility for *all* who want that kind of career. But it isn't. It's heavily loaded in favour of some employees and against others. Being able to 'get in and get on' in our current time culture is highly dependent on our gender, our personal situation and our demographic. It's also dependent on us making sacrifices in terms of our own wellbeing.

And it's not only hurting us: our time culture is hurting businesses too. Research shows that the most diverse and inclusive organizations consistently perform best in their market, delivering quality services to clients and attracting, retaining and developing the most talented employees in a highly competitive labour market. However, our time culture is negatively impacting companies through reduced productivity, wellbeing and diversity. As a nation, the working hours in the United Kingdom are the longest in Europe[2] – or even the world – yet our productivity lags behind. The incidence of stress and mental ill-health has been rising steadily, costing our health services over £22 billion per year[3] and employers over £42 billion per year.[4] As workplaces are failing to meet the needs of different groups of employees, businesses are making glacial progress towards their diversity goals.

When we talk about time and work, we focus almost exclusively on the individual, thinking in terms of what working hours are agreed or expected and how many days' leave we can take, and how many hours we have billed to clients or spent chasing new business. There are countless sources of advice and many thoughtful experts encouraging us as individuals to work smarter and harder, and to be more productive with our time. The overwhelming ethos here is 'it's all about the individual' – but I would argue that it's the *system* we need to fix. We need to stop treating the symptoms and start treating the cause. This means looking critically at how we work, at what we collectively spend our time doing, and asking ourselves: 'Is there a better way – one that works better for each employee and works better for the business?'

By changing our time culture, we can create more sustainable ways of working that will allow all kinds of talent to flourish. Careers will last longer, and richer diversity of thought and experience will lead to better creativity and decision-making. More employees will be able to thrive and succeed, and employers will reap the benefits in terms of attracting and retaining talent and improving business performance.

How this book will help you and your organization

This book reveals the ways in which we undervalue time at work, pinpoints the damaging consequences of this and sets out a compelling alternative. I hope this provokes more open conversations about our time culture at work and encourages debate, experimentation and a collective determination to change the way we work for the better.

Part 1 articulates the burning platform on which we are all standing and the compelling case for change. It explains how our time culture today is a hidden, ticking liability that urgently needs to be addressed by business and HR leaders. Chapter 1 looks at how businesses typically think about time and what's wrong with this. In Chapter 2, we discover why we aren't acknowledging our time failings at work, and how this collective 'time blindness' manifests itself. Its impact is explained in Chapter 3, which lists the typical causes and indicators of 'broken' time and how it affects people in the workplace. We step back in Chapter 4 to look more broadly at the wider social, economic and environmental events and developments influencing our time culture. Chapter 5 sets out the evidence that maintaining the status quo is damaging productivity, wellbeing and diversity, and ultimately business performance, and shows how business and HR leaders can seize a window of opportunity now to create a more time-positive culture.

Part 2 gets practical: it looks closely at what a more time-positive culture might look like and offers numerous examples from a wide range of organizations to inspire you. Chapter 6 introduces better ways of valuing and managing time, while Chapter 7 digs deeper into different aspects of the organization and sets out time-friendly solutions that enable businesses to flourish. Chapter 8 explores the implications for how employers can better manage people and talent, and identifies further time solutions relating to role design, resourcing, attraction, development, career paths, benefits and rewards, and workplace policies. In Chapter 9 we discover how two leading organizations are successfully transforming the way they manage time at work.

Part 3 is action-oriented. It's all about you and your organization: how you can successfully tackle the time culture that's holding your business back. Chapter 10 examines how to diagnose and assess your time defects and get this on the executive agenda. Having secured the commitment to valuing time more strategically, Chapter 11 then sets out different time strategies and guidance for how to prioritize and sequence your change efforts, avoid potential pitfalls and track your progress. Too many ambitious change efforts fail after a well-intentioned start, so the aim of Chapter 12 is to make sure yours doesn't fizzle out too, helping you to sustain momentum and build flexibility into your new time culture so this can evolve as needed in the years ahead. You'll find a variety of tools and resources in the Appendices to help you re-work time in your business; you may wish to work through these in order, or dip in and out of them as and when it suits you.

There's no time to waste, so let's get started!

Part 1
The ticking time bomb

How we're failing to value and manage time at work

Chapter 1
Time today

How we value and treat time in business today

This chapter explores:

- what businesses value today
- how businesses value time
- how we typically think about time at work
- what collective time management is
- the neuroscience of time
- the main characteristics of working time today.

What businesses value today

BEFORE WE TAKE a look at how businesses think about time, let's look at the bigger picture of what they value. What drives most businesses? Or, to put it differently, what defines success for them?

The first answer is obvious: it's money – in the form of revenue generation, profitability and net returns to the business owners, who are typically the shareholders or partners. This focus on financial measures and gains overrides all other aspirations. Obviously, businesses have a responsibility to secure financial stability along with sufficient reserves to draw on during leaner times. Beyond that, the primary aspiration of any business is to safeguard and ideally grow its financial performance year on year, depending on whether the business is in a burgeoning, mature or declining market. Culturally, the pursuit of revenue and profit maximization trumps everything else in our Western capitalist society.

What else? Clients. In order to achieve their financial goals, businesses need to win and retain clients. Offering and delivering innovative products and services is critical for knowledge-based organizations, as is the ability to respond quickly to client demands and to constantly adapt their services to meet clients' changing needs. Developing long-term, profitable relationships with clients is, in general, far more attractive financially to businesses, compared with the much greater cost and risk involved in securing a high proportion of new clients each year.

Third on the 'valued' list is talent. Businesses need employees with the right skills, motivation and commitment to develop those products and services, win clients and build successful relationships with them over time. This means people who can bring creativity and innovative thinking into the business, who have the critical technical and commercial skills required to deliver complex projects and transactions and who – particularly at the senior levels – can bring new clients with them. Today, businesses increasingly value diversity of talent, influenced by a now indisputable body of research showing that those organizations with diverse workforces and leadership teams outperform less diverse organizations on pretty much all major business metrics (revenue growth, profitability, stock market valuations and more).[1]

It's not just creativity, technical expertise and relevant experience that businesses are seeking, though. In recent years, employers have increasingly placed much greater value on 'soft' skills such as interpersonal communication, collaboration, problem-solving, curiosity and adaptability. Proving you can not only deliver in your role, but also understand the bigger picture, contribute to cross-business initiatives and embrace change makes you a far more attractive proposition to employers today.

Why? Because, to conclude our list, businesses value resilience and agility. In a global environment characterized by volatility, uncertainty, complexity and ambiguity (VUCA) businesses need employees who are open to change and willing to adapt their thinking, knowledge and behaviours. This enables the business to respond quickly to unexpected situations and changing priorities.

How businesses value time

If we want to find a better way to collectively manage our time at work, we need to understand how and why time is important or valuable to us. We can't change something to which we're not paying attention, so the first step is to look more closely at what time means to us at work.

Time is money

It's a well-known saying – but what do we really mean here? Let's unpack this. When we say 'time is money', we mean that time represents a cost to the business. For example, the cost of sale: how much it will cost us to pursue a project opportunity or to close a deal? Or the opportunity cost: what potential future gain may be lost as a result of a decision we've made? Time is also a cost in terms of resources (aka employees). What is the total resourcing cost required to deliver client work, and how can this cost stay below the price we're charging to the client so we can generate a profit?

Businesses also assign a financial value to time, typically in a hierarchy of value rather than a fixed or universal value. Two classic examples are reward packages and fee rates. Reward packages assign a value to time by 'buying' a specified number of working hours from an individual over a specified period of time – simply put, your working hours in return for your salary. This concept of time loses meaning in organizations or industries where employees' actual hours worked vastly exceed their contracted hours – a common occurrence in many large, professional firms. With fee rates, an employee's time is charged to the client at a stated price per hour. An hour of a senior employee with more years of career experience and/or more qualifications under their belt is assigned a greater value than an hour of a junior employee, which is where the hierarchy comes in. The commercial practice of 'leverage' involves finding the ideal combination of people's time that will generate the most profits to the firm.

Time is a proxy for 'human capital'

Related to, but not the same as, the concept of 'time is money' in terms of human resources, human capital is a concept coined by eighteenth-century Scottish economist and philosopher Adam Smith to encompass not just the economic value of the work that employees do but also their investments in expanding their knowledge and skills that enable the organization to succeed.

The simplest way for businesses to define their human capital is as the number of employees with different skills and knowledge working full time or part time for their business. They also view human capital in terms of length of service – ideally not too short (expensive to the employer) or too long (stagnation of talent and diversity), but somewhere in between.

Time is presence

For decades, time at work has been associated with being physically present in the office. Working time has been highly synchronous: people show up at roughly the same time to do their work and leave at 'the end of the day'. The gradual rise of 'working from home' over the last decade or two hardly dented this way of valuing time, until the COVID-19 pandemic triggered mass remote working on a scale never anticipated. At the time of writing, it is too soon to tell what the long-term impacts of this will be on Western business time culture – although we will be considering it more throughout the book.

Time is sooner rather than later

In industries that produce tangible products and often require major capital investments, such as manufacturing, pharmaceuticals or oil and gas, 5–10, 10–20 or even 25+ year time horizons are common. In contrast, knowledge-based businesses tend to focus on the nearer term rather than the longer term. They think of time in terms of the working day, week, month, quarter or year. Their business volumes and activity levels are driven by operational cycles, such as results reporting, planning and budgeting processes, and pay and performance reviews. In this culture, the emphasis is much more on the 'here and now'; only senior management and strategy functions are likely to be more focused on the longer-term horizons.

Time is what we measure

'What gets measured, gets managed,' stated Peter Drucker.[2] What we measure, incentivize and reward drives how much time we invest in sales calls, project discussions, client meetings, personal development, compliance activities and so on. If our annual bonus is determined by whether we have met, exceeded or missed our sales target, we will inevitably focus on chasing down sales above everything else. Businesses that recognize this tend to adopt more holistic measurement frameworks to help them evaluate a range of performance outcomes rather than just financial ones. One such example is the balanced scorecard, a tool widely used by senior managers to review progress towards strategic or operational objectives from four different perspectives: financial; customer; internal business processes; and learning and growth.

How we typically think about time at work

Given that businesses are made up of people, how do we *think* about time at work? For all our creativity and inventiveness, we tend to think about time in a surprisingly limited, unchanging way.

First, we think about the number of hours we typically allocate to work in a given day or week. These are shaped by shared 'temporal boundaries': beginnings and ends, and breaks in between. Traditionally, working hours are specified in employment contracts, the classic example being a 40-hour week worked 9.00 am to 5.00 pm each day with working time outside of those boundaries considered overtime. Yet today it is far more common for work hours to be defined as 'to meet the needs of the business', and overtime typically to be unpaid in professional roles.[3] We also think about days off and points in the year where we might take one or two weeks' annual leave at a stretch.

Second, we tend to focus on filling our time with activity. Our work culture is task focused, meaning we prioritize 'getting stuff done', ticking items off our 'to do' lists and meeting deadlines. This culture of busyness is an overwhelming characteristic of modern working life, with the urgent usually taking priority over the important. We'll look a little later at how and why we find meaning in busyness – for now, it suffices to recognize that this social culture exists.

Third, we tend to think about time in relation to individuals and not in terms of a collective group. We put significant effort into managing our *own* time, but think far less about the impact of our time choices and habits on others, and poor time management at a senior level can quickly permeate through the rest of the business. One respondent to a survey about working time that I conducted in November 2020 captured this idea perfectly for me, answering the question about how much time freedom they felt they had with: 'It depends quite a bit on other people's calendars!'

Our concept of time at work is changing

The way we think about time at work is evolving in quite dramatic ways, driven by many factors, including the tools and technology used at work; the rise of dual-career couples; the global nature of many teams; and most notably, in recent times, the impact of the COVID-19 pandemic on the way we work. Here are some examples of how the ways in which we think about time at work have changed over the last few years:

- Remote working and collaboration tools have moved from the fringe to the mainstream. Ten years ago, a few enthusiasts were tentatively trialling online messaging in our consulting firm. Today, businesses everywhere use enterprise-wide collaboration tools, and have massively scaled up their remote working capability.
- With the costs of living, housing and childcare growing faster than average incomes in recent years, in over 70% of couple families in the United Kingdom with dependent children, both partners work.[4] As a result, the need for more flexible working patterns has increased to allow working parents in particular to manage their family commitments alongside their work responsibilities.
- In today's highly networked and global organizations, teams are no longer organized on the basis of a common location, but drawn together from different regions. This means work on a particular project or transaction progresses around the clock, and meetings and calls happen earlier in the morning and later in the evening to accommodate different time zones. As a result, our

temporal boundaries and our mental concept of a working day are constantly expanding.

- The mass remote working triggered by the COVID-19 pandemic has dramatically changed our notions of time at work. For many, time spent on a daily commute has evaporated. Many new remote workers found that boundaries between home time and work time have become more fluid or dissolved completely. As each of us has adapted our working hours (to a greater or lesser extent), working time has become more personalized and less synchronous. We aren't necessarily all in work mode at the same time anymore, and often we're no longer sharing the same start, break and end times as before.

What is collective time management?

These shifts are provoking deeper thinking about how we use our time at work:

- When and why will we bring people physically together in offices in the future?
- What do we most need to use this time for?
- How much autonomy and control over their working time will we give to employees?
- How can we best collaborate across teams and functions when our working time is becoming much more individualized?
- What's the most productive and healthy way for each employee to spend their working hours?
- How can we still find time for fostering personal connections and a strong sense of community when we are geographically dispersed?
- How do we make sure we're investing the same time and effort in managing and developing all employees if we're moving towards new hybrid models of working?

Answering all these questions requires decisions and tradeoffs about how we spend our time: my time, your time, everyone's time. Collective time management is about understanding how we are all spending our time today and making conscious, strategic choices about how we want to be investing our time tomorrow.

It's not about how much we individually achieve each working day or how you or I can manage our own time more efficiently. Those are personal choices and decisions – in other words, individual time management. Collective time management involves taking a systemic view of all those individual time choices and making decisions about our aggregated use of time. Think of it as a 'time piggy bank', where each coin in the piggy bank represents our own working hours. With collective time management, we're looking at the sum of all the coins in the piggy bank and deciding how we are going to invest this valuable resource. Figure 1.1 shows some of the differences between collective and individual time management.

Figure 1.1 Collective vs individual time management

Collective time management	Individual time management
Strategic How we choose to invest our combined time now and over the longer term	**Tactical** How I divide up and use my time during a day or week to achieve certain tasks or meet deadlines
Value-driven Focusing on the important priorities that will help our business to succeed	**Efficiency-driven** Completing my work as efficiently as possible
Shared Creating a time culture that works well for everyone	**Personalized** Making time choices and habits that work best for me
Overall impact What we collectively achieve with our combined use of working time	**My impact** How I can make the best contribution within the working time I have available

How we manage our time collectively is influenced by a number of factors. One major influence is the way an organization is designed: its structure, processes, governance, roles, resourcing and use of technology. We'll take a closer look at this in Chapter 2.

Another major influence is the wider environment in which we work. Chapter 4 shows how global events, societal trends, industry regulations and new technologies shape our collective approach to time.

Another significant influence is the way our human brain functions. Understanding the neuroscience behind the way we think about time is key to building more time awareness and changing our time habits – we'll explore this idea next.

The neuroscience of time

In his book *Thinking Fast and Slow*,[5] the psychologist, economist and Nobel Prize winner Daniel Kahneman explains how the mind works, its incredible functioning and its hidden flaws. He shows how we rely heavily on intuition and automatic responses (our 'fast' thinking) and how effortful but important it is for us to engage in more considered, controlled thinking (our 'slow' thinking). To help it cope with all the demands fired at it, our brain adopts shortcuts known as heuristics and biases. Some of these affect our attitudes and behaviours with regard to time:

- *The novelty bias.* We're easily distracted by our environment and anything 'new', making it hard for us to concentrate for extended periods of time.
- *The over-confidence bias.* We attach too much weight to our intuition and easily recalled information, leading us to jump to conclusions too quickly.
- *The optimism bias.* We're over-optimistic when forecasting, scoping or making assumptions and decisions, resulting in poor planning and unrealistic timeframes.

Separate parts of our brain deal with planning and doing. Additionally, our brains are not well designed for processing time. We rely heavily on selected moments, memories and stories rather than accessing our full range of experiences. And we value time today far more than time tomorrow.[6] These characteristics mean we find it hard to move between managing and completing work; we are prone to making impaired judgements; and we tend to overestimate our available time and overcommit ourselves.

We can learn from this, and it helps to realize what our brains like and don't like in relation to time. Our brains work best, for example, when we have high autonomy and control over our time and the way we do our work.[7] We also gain satisfaction and pleasure from our ability to complete tasks promptly without distractions. Setting temporal boundaries – where we segment our working day into blocks of time with defined start and end points – helps our brain to function efficiently. The same applies to breaking up large and/or long-term projects into smaller chunks of work. This 'chunking' makes it easier for our brain to identify, store and retrieve memories. Our brains also benefit from periods of inactivity and rest to allow them to sort, process and categorize all the incoming information they have been receiving. Taking short pauses frequently during the day can help us to gain perspective, generate new ideas and work more efficiently. Daydreaming, far from being a waste of time, returns our brain to its natural resting state and resets our emotions.

On the other hand, being engaged in a constant mental sprint under time pressure causes our brain to burn through fuel and become cognitively overloaded. Multitasking is far from being the hyper-efficient mode of operating that we have traditionally celebrated. It speeds up the production of cortisol, the stress hormone, and adrenaline, the fight-or-flight hormone. This makes us feel mentally overstimulated and, over time, cognitively depleted. In this state, we lurch unknowingly into superficial or poorly evaluated decision-making. Too much effort is required to consider Donald Rumsfeld's famous 'unknown unknowns'[8] – unidentified risks or possibilities so unexpected that we cannot even conceive of them – so it is much easier to base our decisions on the limited information in front of us. Our mood is negatively impacted by frequent interruptions and other visual and auditory disturbances. Our impulse control gets weaker, making it harder for us to focus on the task at hand and resist the lure of the dopamine feedback loops that reward distractions. Our impaired self-control can also make it harder for us to stop working and switch off at the end of a hectic, full day.

The good news is that we can mitigate some of these shortcuts and biases and create a healthier, more productive mindset regarding time by adopting some of the following habits, taken from Daniel Levitin's fascinating book *The organized mind*:[9]

- *Creating calm environments:* ways of working and physical spaces that reduce interruptions, help us get into 'flow' and stay on task.
- *Limiting our working hours:* our productivity declines dramatically with overwork, even though we misguidedly believe we are achieving more.
- *Taking power naps:* just five or ten minutes can help us improve our memories and power of recall, recalibrate our emotions, and help our brain to function more productively.
- *Tackling the important and/or less enticing tasks first, otherwise known as 'eating the frog':* our willpower depletes during the day,[10] so by addressing our tendency to procrastinate, we can conserve more energy.
- *Batch processing:* clustering similar chores together helps us to get more done and feel less exhausted.
- *Finding time together:* being part of a group and maintaining our social connections is neurologically proven to give us comfort and a sense of belonging.

The main characteristics of working time today

Having looked at how we think about time as both businesses and people, and having covered the neuroscience of how our brains deal with time at work, what is the main trend we can observe about working time today? In short, we're spending increasing amounts of time at/on work.

For many of us, the length of our working day or week bears little resemblance to the time-old phrase of '9 to 5', or the concept of work time as set out in the Working Time Regulations of 1998 (updated in 2003). These specify a maximum average of 48 hours to be worked per week over a 17-week period with a minimum of 24 hours' rest in any seven-day period unless the employee 'opts out', which the majority in professional roles and firms are 'invited' to do by their employer. So what is the reality hidden behind the idea of the 9 to 5 work day?

Many of us work more hours than we are contracted or paid for. More than five million UK workers put in a total of two billion unpaid hours' work in 2018,[11] an average of 7.5 hours per week per person. Those in managerial and professional occupations tend to have more opportunities to work flexibly, but also work longer hours[12] overall. One study of 1500 professionals in the City of London found that 91% worked beyond their contracted hours on a weekly basis, and almost half (43%) did not leave the office or take a break at lunchtime. In fact, we're spending so much time at work that national initiatives and campaigns such as Work Your Proper Hours Day[13] and Go Home on Time Day[14] have sprung up and are being supported by many employers. We're also too busy to take all our annual leave: 40%[15] of us don't take all our leave entitlement for this very reason.

Of course, it would be foolish to ignore the event with perhaps the greatest single impact on work – as well as the rest of life and the world – the COVID-19 pandemic. The worst global pandemic in living memory has – along with the myriad and as yet untold impacts on the world – changed our pattern of work hours. Although at the time of writing the pandemic is not truly over and the long-term implications are yet to be seen, already it is fair to say that this has been a paradigm-shifting event in many ways. In one global study[16] published in September 2020, half of employees said they'd been working either the same or more hours regularly since the start of the pandemic. A July 2020 study[17] of 3.1 million workers across North America, Europe and the Middle East found 'significant and durable increases in the length of the average workday' during lockdowns.

However, despite these longer work days during lockdowns – or perhaps because of them – more working time is being lost. Yes, that's right: alongside this inexorable rise in work hours we are seeing a corresponding rise in lost productivity. We're taking more days off than ever before due to work-related ill-health. Some 17.9 million working days[18] were lost due to work-related stress, depression or anxiety in Great Britain in 2019/20. Each affected individual took an average of 21.6 days off, and cases were highest in professional and technical occupations and in larger workplaces.[19]

Sleep deprivation is affecting our productivity too. Research[20] conducted in 2016 showed that insufficient sleep was costing the United Kingdom over $50 billion per year (£36 billion per year) in economic losses as a result of over 200,000 working days lost per year.

In addition to all this, we feel more 'time poor'. Thanks to our tendency to focus on working and making money above all else, the phenomenon of time poverty is well entrenched in our society. We're all endlessly busy, with never enough leisure or downtime – even when we enjoy some time flexibility in our work lives. But why are we so busy? On the plus side, holding down a demanding job gives many people a sense of purpose and achievement in our status-driven culture. However, most people are driven to work hard not by the sense of fulfilment they get, but by a combination of less enticing factors, including the rise of job insecurity, the escalating costs of housing and education, and less generous pension terms than 15 years ago. On top of that, parents (at least in wealthy nations) are spending more time with their children than ever before[21] – meaning that time spent not at work and not with children is left practically non-existent.

This time poverty is also reflected in the rising prevalence of loneliness, including loneliness in the workplace. A study[22] in March 2020 – even before the global pandemic saw many of us confined to our homes – found that three in five people feel lonely at work. Tellingly, 44% attributed this to work pressure, while 42% linked it to 'not fitting in'. These findings should be a red flag for employers: 68% of those who felt lonely at work said it had increased their stress levels and 38% said it had negatively affected their productivity.

Houston, we have a problem

Overworking. Busyness. Time poverty. Bad habits. Poor decision-making. Already the problematic nature of our relationship with time at work is emerging. In the next chapter, let's dig deeper into why we're not attentive to the way we manage time at work. What aren't we talking about, and why?

Chapter 2
Time blindness

Why we have developed time 'blind spots' in the workplace

This chapter explores:

- our time blindness affliction
- how time is deeply embedded in our world of work
- norms about time at work
- technology: friend or foe?
- where time blindness leads.

Our time blindness affliction

LET ME INTRODUCE you to the concept of time blindness. This is our collective failure to notice, acknowledge and debate our habits and choices about the way we spend our working time.

This time blindness has three main characteristics:

1. *accepting* without questioning that the way we've always treated time at work is the only way to treat it

2. *believing* that time management is solely a matter for the individual

3. *conforming* to group think and behavioural norms regarding the ways we talk about – and don't talk about – time.

Why aren't we talking about time blindness? First, we talk about time in a very limited way. We're comfortable talking about milestones, deadlines, working hours, business cycles, process design and efficiencies. We talk far less, however, about our priorities, choices and tradeoffs regarding *how we spend* our time. As one expert put it to me in conversation, 'This isn't a discussed phenomenon where people are talking about how time gets used, how they can manage their day, what they choose to prioritize and to not prioritize. Time doesn't seem to be something that gets talked about.'

Second, time goes unacknowledged in many ways. There isn't a Department in charge of Time Management or a Head of Time. Yet many companies choose to have functions and roles for other intangible aspects of the organization, such as heads of culture, diversity, risk, efficiency, wellbeing, employee experience and even happiness. Similarly, how we manage time doesn't tend to be mentioned in business objectives, organizational metrics or performance targets. It may get raised in organizations that explicitly discuss productivity – but many organizations don't do this.

Third, we don't routinely analyse what we're collectively spending our time on. Large amounts of data relating to time may be gathered, but it's often at the individual level or team level, or for a very specific purpose – for example, time spent cold-calling potential clients, time spent on learning and development activities or time set aside annually for corporate social responsibility (CSR) initiatives.

Fourth, we're used to starting new initiatives and taking on new responsibilities, and far less accustomed to stopping activities and relinquishing responsibilities. In this way, we're treating time as if it is endlessly elastic, not something that is finite that we have to weigh up and negotiate over.

How often do we hear leaders saying 'I want you to stop spending time on…' and explaining why? Like politicians, business leaders are full of excitement to announce new initiatives. It's understandable: it is far less exciting to announce the cancellation or postponement of activity – indeed, in many cases it's seen as tantamount to confessing that we might have wasted time and money unnecessarily.

Which leads onto the fifth reason. We're not good at admitting to wasted time. It reflects badly on us as individuals because businesses value competence, achievement and results. So it can feel countercultural and career-limiting to even question why we are spending time on certain activities.

Employers have been able to get away with complacency, until now. Time might be a finite resource, but people seemingly aren't. If someone leaves the organization because the work demands on their time are unhealthy, unsustainable or incompatible with their home/personal lives, the employer can always just hire another worker to fill the gap.

In a competitive world where job security is both precious and scarce, people will go to great lengths to demonstrate their value to their employer and hold onto their jobs. This means they will often absorb the extra working hours required and sacrifice their own time in the interests of going the extra mile for the business. Consciously or unconsciously, employers have let employees take on this burden of 'time buffering'. They have left it to individuals to stretch their personal boundaries of working time to breaking point and then, when the reality of multiple stress-related absences and burnout becomes impossible to ignore, they line up wellbeing seminars, gym memberships and mindfulness sessions to help people cope. This is the sticking plaster approach. It literally covers up the real problem – our failure to manage working time effectively – and hides it from view so we're not seeing it for what it is or talking about it. We'll see in Chapter 5 why businesses can no longer afford to ignore this problem.

Our time blindness is also genuinely difficult to assess and address. It isn't a standalone, isolated problem that can easily be rectified with a one-dimensional solution or some tinkering around the edges while the rest of the organization steams ahead unchanged. It's a systemic issue that has evolved over decades of organizational behaviour and is hiding in plain sight. Our approach to time is completely wrapped up in the way we discuss, plan, organize and deliver our work. It touches every aspect of our organization: how businesses are structured, the goals we set, the roles we create, the appointments we make, the tools, processes and procedures we adopt, our shared values and behaviours.

Time is deeply embedded in our world of work

Time is woven into our experience of work from the minute we think about joining an organization. When jobs are advertised, time is referenced in the selection criteria, typically as the number of years of industry experience or technical expertise required from applicants. A significant amount of time is invested in the recruitment process by both recruiter and candidate, with long and multi-stage recruitment processes common. The average time taken to hire a successful candidate is 27.5 days, rising to 30 days in financial services and 38 days in professional services firms.[1] This 'time to hire' and the length of time the new hire stays at the company are the two primary recruitment metrics[2] used by firms to evaluate the success of their recruitment efforts. Time clauses abound in employment contracts, specifying working-time requirements and time-off entitlements. In recent years, the campaign to offer more time-flexible contracts has gathered pace, with more employers adopting the #happytotalkflexibleworking[3] strapline and logo.

Once we're through the door, time is hard-wired into the way people are managed. Performance objectives and assessment typically follow an annual cycle, as do salary and bonus reviews and awards. Performance metrics often include targets in terms of hours spent on certain activities. Employment benefits are largely defined in time increments: from the number of days' leave offered for various purposes to the number of days of training or continuous professional development the employee is encouraged/expected to fulfil. Career paths are typically linear, with progression up the career ladder often defined by the amount of time spent in certain roles or at certain levels along the way. Time out from the world of work is typically viewed with suspicion by employers, and can disadvantage job candidates unless they can demonstrate how purposefully this time has been invested.

Time is woven into the way businesses are led and managed. Planning horizons and budgeting, forecasting and reporting cycles all dictate an organization's operating rhythm. Business performance is typically benchmarked and assessed relative to the results of previous quarters, half-years or years. Resourcing decisions – how people are allocated onto different projects or initiatives – are usually based on the number of hours' or days' input required, as well as the skills and expertise needed. Most large organizations rely on predominantly centralized structures for decision-making. This requires time for data, information and recommendations to flow upwards to senior levels in order for decisions to be made, and more time for those decision outcomes to be communicated back out to the wider organization.

Meanwhile, our own working time is sucked up by a metaphorical vacuum in myriad different ways. When we start work each day, we hit the ground running, straight into task completion or interaction modes. Our working time has become highly fragmented as we switch frequently between multiple priorities, responsibilities and different types of work activities during any given day. In parallel, the time it takes us to do our work has both sped up and slowed down. Response times and deadlines have shortened thanks to modern technology and competition, but information overload means it takes us longer to identify the specific information we need. Similarly, organizational complexity has led to more re-working and iteration of proposals as multiple stakeholders need to be consulted and work documents are repeatedly reviewed and revised.

Time is not only embedded into our organizational structures, processes and information flows: it is also deeply woven into our assumptions and the social norms that underpin the way we work.

Norms about time at work

A social norm is an expected way of behaving or doing things that most people agree with. Often these are not verbalized or written down anywhere, but in organizations they have a powerful influence on our work culture, including the way we spend our time. Here are some common time norms I have observed, heard about and researched during my career.

It's all urgent

Our working hours are crammed full. We are driven to work faster and smarter in order to stay on top of multiple responsibilities and deadlines. In doing so, we frequently fall into the trap of focusing on the most urgent tasks at the expense of the important ones. How often have you started your day resolved to complete an important piece of work, only to be side-tracked by an urgent request (or several) from your boss or a colleague? Or from a client, which in many people's experience is even harder to say no to.

I need to respond now

This urgency means we quickly lapse into reactive mode. We spend too much time responding to incoming demands rather than preserving our mental energy and time for more productive, creative or strategic work. In a survey I conducted in November 2020, I asked respondents to rank different types of work activities according to average amount of time they spent on them each week. People spent the most time 'dealing with incoming demands day to day', closely followed by 'participating in calls and meetings'. 'Doing deep thinking/productive/creative work alone' came last, and for many 'the real work gets done outside of working hours'.

I'll have time later

Most of us are guilty of squandering our time at work, distracted by our surroundings, checking emails or social media, or procrastinating when starting a piece of work. As working hours have lengthened and work–home boundaries have dissolved, it's easy to assume we'll get round to doing tasks later in the day. As one survey respondent commented mournfully, 'there are no hard stops any more'. Yet part-time employees, working parents and carers are often the most productive during their working hours precisely because they invariably have a hard stop.

We need a meeting

Our work culture is intensively meeting heavy, and our discipline around meeting management is often woeful. Meetings are routinely scheduled for an hour (or more), run back to back, lack a clear agenda and output, and are inefficiently chaired. Furthermore, many participants are in listening mode only.

Busy is good, idle is bad

Downtime at work for any reason – reading, reflection, stepping away to gain perspective, taking breaks, chatting with others – tends to be labelled as unproductive time. Being lost in thought looks like idling. Time spent on purely social conversations is not viewed as being as valuable or as purposeful as work-focused activity. The accepted norm is to appear busy because this sends the signal that we are productive, important and achieving great things.

Full-time gets you further

Full-time contracts are still the predominant model of employment at 63%, while part-time contracts have grown slowly to 26%. But if you want to get to senior positions, working part time isn't always going to help you achieve this. The number of years worked part time is inversely correlated to progression,[4] and in 2020 only 3.6% of roles earning over £80,000 per annum were held by part-timers.[5] Why? A pervasive 'out of sight, out of mind' attitude still exists in our work culture. As explained by a senior business leader, 'A partner who works three days a week is constantly worried about opportunities passing them by because they are not working on Mondays and Fridays. I have to be on guard to make sure that they don't get left out of stuff. Because that is what happens when you're not around. It goes to somebody else.'

We fill up tomorrow fast

We tend to value our future time less than our time today. So we say 'yes' more often to requests that require our time in the future, then realize too late that we've overcommitted. Additionally, we're happy to rely on intuition over evidence when planning and scoping, but this frequently leads us to be overconfident in our estimates – remember Kahneman's research?

My time matters more than yours

We are often mindful when it comes managing our own time, but tend to be far less cognizant of the impact of our own choices and decisions on other people's time. While it might suit us to fire off several emails early in the morning before others are online, we don't pause to think about how that might feel for the recipients(s) opening up a freshly filled inbox. Requesting last-minute revisions may mean a colleague is forced to work late. We routinely accommodate these behaviours without asking whether there is a better way.

Technology: friend or foe?

Has technology contributed to our time blindness? Or is it helping us to collectively value and manage our time better? Yes, and yes – like so many things, technology is not purely harmful or purely helpful.

Today's tools that enable remote working, team collaboration, knowledge management and communications have removed much of our need to be physically present in an office in order to participate in meetings, access and share information, or work on deliverables together. As a result, many knowledge-based workers have more choice and control over when and where they work than before. The great benefit this brings is the ability to tailor our working hours and location in a way that helps us to manage our life outside of work.

We are also able to reach out to colleagues around the world who have the knowledge we need to draw upon. Intranets, online communities and workplace messaging tools help us to find and connect easily with others who can share valuable expertise and experience. In bringing together diverse talents and perspectives, we can robustly test our ideas and develop well-rounded solutions at speed. We can work more efficiently too. When we're skilled at using the technology and tools at our disposal (and when that technology is reliable), we're able to work more autonomously and rely less on others to complete tasks for us. Instead of asking a graphic expert to produce our slides, a research expert to design a survey or a website manager to update a webpage, we can do it ourselves.

So far, so good. But all this information at our fingertips and all these tools at our disposal often lead to overload, complexity, inefficiency and exclusive rather than inclusive behaviours.

We don't always use or organize our technology in a way that helps us to make the best use of our time. Ever-expanding quantities of information 'out there' mean it has to be exceedingly well structured and signposted for us to quickly find what we need. We can spend hours trying to track down the right version of a document, wade through emails trying to locate a comment we spotted yesterday, or click through multiple intranet pages to find an answer to a problem. It isn't always clear what tool or communication channel we should use for what purpose. We tend to over-rely on email for multiple purposes, leading to legendary email volumes that are impossible to manage.

Our over-reliance on technology can lead to unintentionally exclusive behaviours. If we throw an idea 'out there' for reactions, it's far too easy to move to a decision or action when we've received a few speedy responses from those colleagues who happen to be online at the same time. By missing other perspectives, we are closing down opportunities for debate and constructive challenge, and rushing to potentially hasty decisions. Then we can waste hours across our working week through a host of 'time sinks'. These are low-value activities that drain our productive time, such as retrieving information, rectifying poor quality data, making poor use of the short periods of time between meetings and switching our attention between a variety of tasks rather than 'batch processing' similar tasks.

We are increasingly aware of the negative impact of technology on our wellbeing, particularly at work. Not only do multitasking and attentional switching overload our cognitive functioning, but many of us struggle to switch off from our addictively designed devices and take proper breaks. The enforced remote working experienced by many during the COVID-19 pandemic required many people to spend large portions of their day interacting online, which is mentally and physically draining. From this evolved new phenomena such as the so-called 'tyranny of the green light', as described by a senior HR leader: 'Is your green light on in Microsoft Teams? This tells other people whether you're there or not and in order to be regarded as contributing, your green light has to be on.'

By equating time spent online with productive time, we have simply exchanged office-based presenteeism – a problem we touched on in the previous chapter – with e-presenteeism.

Where does time blindness lead?

Let's return to our definition of time blindness: our collective failure to notice, acknowledge and debate our combined habits and choices about the way we are spending our time at work. Now we have understood more about this affliction, we can start to explore some of the symptoms that it triggers. What situations and set-ups are we stumbling into as a result? How does it affect the way organizations function? What are the tell-tale signs that time blindness is at work in your organization? In the next chapter we'll look more closely at these 'time defects'.

Chapter 3
Time defects

The signs and impact of 'broken' time in organizations

This chapter explores:

- common time defects
- how these defects are impacting different groups of employees
- how broken time is damaging inclusion.

Our time blindness isn't a harmless condition. Like blind spots when driving, it can be downright dangerous. Time blindness causes flaws and dysfunctions in the way we operate, and these 'defects' prevent us from collectively delivering our best work. They also create barriers that make it harder for people to bring their whole selves to work and to flourish in their careers.

Common time defects

THESE TIME DEFECTS have gradually evolved as our organizations have expanded and contracted, adopted new processes and technologies, and adapted to changing market conditions and pressures. We have learned to accommodate the defects unquestioningly as a necessary feature of working life. Occasionally they are thrown into sharp relief by external crises such as economic downturns, environmental disasters or pandemics.

Here are eight examples of time defects that occur in organizations. We'll look at each of them in turn:

1. governance imbalances
2. growth-at-all-costs leadership
3. process overload
4. distracting environments
5. vanishing boundaries
6. lack of control
7. input fixation
8. career traps.

Governance imbalances

Many board members and business leaders bemoan the excessive time involved in preparing and digesting lengthy pre-meeting papers. In the words of one HR leader:

> If I just went in to talk to the board about [the plan], I wouldn't have to write it; my boss wouldn't have to read it; my other boss wouldn't have to rewrite it for me because they like it in their words, not mine; the board wouldn't have to pre-read it. We'd just have a discussion about it. But there's this constant need for masses and masses of documentation around everything. It's a complete waste of time.

This time drain is borne out by a 2017 study[1] which found board members spent on average just under four hours reading their papers for each meeting, up 30% in six years. More than half their packs consisted of 200+ pages and some a staggering 1000 pages.

How much more focused and effective could board discussions be with more time-sensitive briefings? Lack of time for debate is one of the risk factors contributing to poor decision-making identified by the Financial Reporting Council (FRC), the corporate governance regulator in the United Kingdom and Ireland.

But it isn't just about time as an input into board decisions. It's also about the time horizons for their decision-making. The FRC advises that 'boards have a responsibility for the health of the company and need to take a long-term view. This is in contrast to the priorities of some investors, not all of whom will be aligned with the pursuit of success over the longer-term.'[2] One chair of a FTSE 100 company stressed to me the importance of good environmental, social and governance (ESG) practices over short-term profit maximization. However, the tension between the long-term interests of all stakeholders and the more immediate concerns of investors still too often lands in favour of the latter. As a senior director in the investment industry explained, 'Investors aren't really looking more long-term. Companies are still under pressure from their shareholders to meet this year's earnings expectations, to push up next year's earnings expectations and then beat those.'

Growth-at-all-costs leadership

In our Western culture, leaders are often narrowly focused on priorities that drive *growth* – in terms of size, revenue, client base and profits – rather than sustainability. In professional services, firms try to bill as many hours as they can to each client, with the primary goal of maximizing partner profits at the end of the year. These aren't the actions of long-term owners valuing stakeholder interests. Interestingly, though, this one-dimensional ethos may be starting to change. Early signs show that one result of the COVID-19 pandemic is that many firms have been encouraged to rethink their purpose in broader terms. For example, the incoming CEO of Herbert Smith Freehills, an elite international law firm, stated in an interview[3] that one of his top three priorities was to develop longer-term client relationships that were less transactional and more based on empathy.

So, in a growth-at-all-costs culture, do leaders regularly look at how time is being invested across their business and question their own use of time? Not exactly. The closest that leadership teams get to this is when they agree their quarterly priorities. They might acknowledge the need to question time spent on non-priority activities. But the discipline required to keep checking on this is often lacking, according to executive coaches I've interviewed. This is compounded by the huge investment of personal time and energy that many business leaders dedicate to their jobs. One executive coach described this as 'a sort of Faustian contract… that seems to go with the territory'. A head-hunter confirmed that executive selection criteria are skewed in favour of high-energy people able to devote all their waking hours to the organization. This practice inevitably sustains a widespread belief that getting to the top requires superhuman energy levels and the sacrificing of outside interests and relationships. It doesn't promote a healthy time culture.

Process overload

In businesses today, a plethora of processes, initiatives and programmes are in play at any one time. Some are ongoing 'business as usual' processes (research, marketing, delivery of client work, financial management, compliance, people management and so on), while others are more finite in duration (transformation projects, new tools and technology, updates to HR policies, etc.). Whatever their nature, these processes usually have different 'owners' and are led by different functions.

The problem is that there is rarely somebody overseeing all these different processes or looking at their combined impact on employees. No one has the task of assessing the time required to execute the different stages of any process. Consequently, employees frequently find themselves being pulled in multiple directions and put under pressure to satisfy competing demands on their time. This is both inefficient and unrealistic from a time perspective; one professional commented to me that their biggest time drain was 'feeding into business processes that don't add value to my work'.

In addition to these major business processes, many respondents in my work time survey[4] commented on the substantial time they devoted each week to routine tasks and essential compliance activities. As organizations have cut costs and become leaner, administrative and technical support has decreased and self-service tools have mushroomed. This has pushed responsibility onto professionals in front line roles for a whole raft of tasks, including diary management, travel bookings, collating information, time and expense submissions, updating status reports and spreadsheets, resolving IT issues, HR data entry and many others. 'Having to do repetitive admin tasks that could be delegated' was a common refrain in survey participants' comments.

Distracting environments

Doing our best work requires an environment – physical and virtual – that helps us concentrate on the task at hand and that minimizes distractions tugging at our attention. While often plush, corporate offices are not always designed to help their occupants to concentrate. Open-plan offices tend to be stuffed full of visual and auditory stimuli and well-meaning colleagues (or our bosses) wander over for a quick chat. We can't blame it all on noise or visual distractions; some of it is down to our own behaviour. While side-chatting with our neighbours is good for social connection and mental breaks, we're prone to habits that unintentionally dent our motivation and concentration. A classic example is complaining. Studies[5] have found that most employees spend 10 or more hours per month complaining – or listening to others complain – about their bosses or senior management. Astonishingly, almost a third spend 20 hours or more doing so. By not raising the issue directly with the party concerned, we are whittling away productive time and fostering discontent.

We can't blame it all on distracting offices: working from home still leaves us with virtual interruptions to contend with. Many professionals say they are unable to switch their instant messaging functionality off; they can only indicate they are 'in a meeting'. Yet they are still bombarded by messages popping up on their screen while on calls or concentrating on their work. One senior professional described it as 'the bane of my life', likening it to 'one of your children popping in saying, "Mummy, can you do this? Can you do that?"'. Add a real child or children at home into the mix, and the chances of uninterrupted work nosedives further, especially for women. Research[6] during the first UK lockdown found that mothers were only able to do one hour of uninterrupted work for every three hours done by fathers.

Vanishing boundaries

Remember when we used to leave our work behind when we left the office and could enjoy a proper break during the evenings, weekends and holidays? Now, thanks to mobile devices, remote access and a highly competitive jobs market, we regularly check emails, hold calls and catch up on work outside of our official working hours. Traditional boundaries between work and home lives are fast dissolving. The technology that has enabled us to 'work from anywhere' has led us to 'work from everywhere'. We're not switching off anymore.

A 2014 survey[7] found that 60% of those who used smartphones were connected to work for 13.5 hours or more a day. Four in 10 managers in Britain put in more than 60 hours a week. This culture of overworking is pointless. After a certain point, productivity actually goes down when the number of hours worked per week goes up. Above 45 hours, productivity drops off a cliff, particularly for knowledge workers. A 60-hour work week, while 50% longer than a 40-hour work week, actually *reduces productivity*[8] by 25%. Overworking is also unhealthy: if you regularly work 55 hours a week or more, you are 35% more likely to suffer a stroke and 17% more likely to die from heart disease[9] than colleagues working 35 to 40 hours per week.

Overworking worsened during the COVID-19 pandemic. In one study, 52% agreed that boundaries between their work and home lives were increasingly blurred, up from 40% in just six months. One consulting partner confided, 'My hours have gone up. I used to work about 50 hours a week. Now I work more, between 55 and 65 on a regular basis. I don't do 70 because I know I'd be falling over.' A senior HR leader agreed, saying 'talk tends to be about working at weekends because the week has been full of (online) meetings'. E-presenteeism dominated, particularly for younger workers: 63%[10] of 18- to 24-year-olds regularly checked their emails outside working hours, up from 48%. While we're all responsible for resisting the lure of our addictive devices, in our speeded-up world it has become the norm to email others at any time of day or night and expect a prompt response.

Lack of control

A defining characteristic of many professionals' work lives is their lack of control over the demands on their time and corresponding lack of time freedom – something identified as a key need for the brain. A study of almost 3000 managers by the Norwegian Business School[11] found that 61.8% 'experienced time pressure often or all the time'. Fewer than 5% said they rarely or never had time pressure at work. Time pressure is due in part to workload and job design, but it's also due to other people's demands on you. Middle and junior managers are rarely able to push back on senior people's demands on their time. As one senior manager explained to me:

while you are the project manager of your own time, you don't have control over other people's time. You're constantly stretched. You might spend a whole day in meetings because other people think that their time and what they're doing is more important. But when you walk away you realize you haven't achieved any of your objectives for that day.

In my own time survey,[12] 59% of respondents reported 'limited' or 'partial' time freedom compared with 40% who enjoyed 'significant' or 'unlimited' time freedom. And we know that time control matters. The same Norwegian study found that managers who feel they have control of their work situation and freedom to make decisions experience *less* work pressure, *less* emotional strain and *considerably less* role stress than managers who lack such control – just as we saw in Chapter 1 when we looked at the neuroscience.

Input fixation

We are too hung up on time as an input – how much time we spend doing X or Y activities. Many of the constructs we use in our businesses use time as the underlying metric because it is convenient. Instead, we should be more focused on the end result, asking ourselves 'What have we actually achieved? What value or impact have we created for our clients, our colleagues, our business and the wider community?' Take client billing, for example. We're stuck in a mental model which says we're selling our time. We charge for the days we show up, or the hours and minutes spent on client work, not for the results our work helps to bring about in our clients' businesses. We struggle to resource part-time colleagues onto projects as these are invariably costed on the basis of full-time resourcing.

Likewise, HR policies typically use time as the basic metric of benefits and entitlements. Consider parental leave. Between maternity, paternity and shared parental leave policies, the employee has to grapple with a mind-boggling complexity of rules surrounding the time off they are allowed, how it may be taken and what limits on eligibility apply. The consequence? There's low awareness, understanding and sometimes take-up. By focusing on time, policies assume everyone's needs are identical and end up being exclusive – working for some but not all – rather than inclusive.

So why don't we simply switch our focus, looking at outputs instead of inputs? Because it is *much harder* to articulate, measure and evaluate outcomes. It is so much easier to stick with measuring time as a proxy. But it's not impossible to change our mindset and practices. Part 2 describes how we can do this, and I'd argue that it is well worth making the difficult shift.

Career traps

When it comes to incentives – financial and career-related – we're rewarding people for their short-term actions and failing to take a longer-term perspective. Most business models and pay strategies are driven by near-term financial goals. Annual bonuses are often determined by the extent to which employees have missed, met or exceeded targets for hours billed and/or revenue generated. In banks, which operate on even shorter-term horizons than professional services firms, forced performance rankings instil a highly competitive culture and 'the fear of being fired', reinforcing a continued focus on immediate results.

With career progression, we are not offering clear and varied options or illustrating the consequences of different choices. As one investment director explained:

> You can very easily fall into being a career analyst unless you make the right moves early on. But in your twenties, nobody tells you that 10 years later you are never going to run a portfolio because you've had too limited experience. It's down to luck not judgment.

While running professional networks in London, I frequently heard people bemoan the one-size-fits-all career paths available. These are typically linear, with progression based on time spent at each level and few alternative routes to the top, and rarely flexed to accommodate different life stages.

For employees whose backgrounds and profiles mirror those of senior leaders, these career paths are obvious and achievable. For others, 'the pathway to the top is unclear, with confusion over which job to seek out at what point in a career'.[13] Even when enlightened, many employees are not able to benefit from spending enough time with senior sponsors and leaders to foster the right connections and build professional networks. This is particularly true for employees of colour, flexible workers, working parents (particularly mothers), carers, LGBTQ+ employees and those with disabilities.

How these defects are impacting different groups of employees

So we've seen eight ways in which our time blindness can hinder effective functioning in organizations. How does that affect people's experiences at work? Research into the effects of time pressure by Leeds University offers some initial clues, confirming that 'people often feel there are insufficient hours in the day and that they have to work longer and harder than ever before. This leads to feelings of time pressure which, in work contexts, have led to employee dissatisfaction, alienation, low productivity and absenteeism.'[14] How does this affect people's career ambitions and decisions? Is the impact the same for everyone or does it vary? Let's dig a little deeper into the consequences of these time defects.

Younger employees

If you've succeeded in overcoming intense competition to land an entry-level role at any large professional employer, you've done exceedingly well. You'll likely be offered a variety of work experiences, a structured development programme and the opportunity to gain valuable business skills. All for enviable pay levels. The downside?

> There's this real idea that you should devote your life to your role. If you want to get ahead you have to be better, you have to be on 24-hour call.

> There's always loads of distractions and nobody guides you on how to prioritize.

These words from two professionals reflecting back on their early roles highlight the real consequences of our time culture for people starting out in their careers. To fit in and get on, analysts, associates and graduate trainees work long hours, juggle many different projects and often have to study for stressful professional exams. The risk of burnout is very real, and has become extreme in some cases: in Japan, the phenomenon of death by overwork, known as *karoshi*,[15] is well documented. But research published in *The Lancet*[16] confirms this happens all around the world, not just in Japan. A tragic example from August 2013 involved a Bank of America Merrill Lynch intern named Moritz Erhardt working in London; he was found dead in his shower after working for 72 hours straight. Since then, some – but not all – banks have imposed restrictions on the number of hours interns can work.

While entry-level roles and development may be well structured, they may also be narrowly defined, limiting networking opportunities and reinforcing hierarchies. I have sat in countless client meetings where the junior team members present are not expected or invited to speak, despite having spent hours contributing to the work being discussed. The COVID-19 pandemic exacerbated these experiences for many younger professionals: e-presenteeism was highest among 18- to 25-year-olds; they were more likely to experience anxiety[17] and to rank their mental health as bad; just one in 10 felt that their employer really understood them; and almost a quarter felt isolated from colleagues.

Parents

Working parents experience different issues as a result of these time defects. Consider the sheer logistical challenge of focusing on your job while managing drop-offs, pick-ups, childcare emergencies, child sickness, teenage pressures and exam stress. Working hours are completely out of kilter with school days and terms, and with dual-career couples now the norm among two-parent households, parents are constantly negotiating their way between work, parenting and domestic commitments. In the words of a few professionals with children:

> It's very difficult for people [at work] to see that you have it in you to give more to your company when you've got this huge distraction at home that you're dealing with, day in, day out. These are well-known reasons why it's really hard to progress.

> Motherhood really changed it for me. I was scared to step back into consulting because I didn't want my job to stop me from being the kind of mother I wanted to be. So I asked for a demotion; [I decided] no, I'm not going to deal with all that anymore. I'm just going to shrink my career ambitions back a bit.

> I'm ambitious but I have to operate differently to other colleagues. I have to adapt my working week to survive.

No wonder so many parents decide to press pause, switch to less demanding roles or exit their professional careers completely.

Then there are those who need fertility support to start or grow their family: over 3.5 million people[18] in the United Kingdom, from those in their twenties through to those in their fifties, including single parents, same-sex couples, and men and women, are experiencing reproductive health issues. The demands on their time, emotions and wallets are significant, and sometimes extreme. Yet companies rarely provide financial support, let alone dedicated time off for attending appointments, undergoing procedures or coping with the stresses and sadness involved.

Employees of colour

Here are some words from one senior female black professional working in the banking sector:

> The workforce today is built for white middle-class males, who may have a wife or nanny at home looking after the baby, and have come from a conventional background. As far back as I can remember, my mother always told us that we have to work 10 times harder than our white peers. That for us to get to those higher positions, we have to do 10 times more than those who don't look or sound like us. We've always been taught that we have to do more with the same time – be more productive, more efficient.

She's not alone. Race research and diversity statistics confirm this experience is shared by many people of colour:

- People of colour struggle to achieve the same progression opportunities as their white counterparts.[19]
- In the United Kingdom, black employees are the most likely to have to wait for three years or more for a promotion (31% vs 23% of white employees[20]).
- In law, solicitors of colour experience lower levels of wellbeing and higher levels of stress, due in part to feeling the need to have to work harder and longer than their white colleagues in order to be accepted and recognized, and to progress.[21]
- Only 38% of black employees said they were satisfied with their career progression to date, compared with 47% of white employees.[22]

How, specifically, do time defects contribute to these career barriers? Here are three examples of how people's careers are impacted negatively:

1. Leaders and colleagues spend insufficient time listening to the experiences of people of colour at work and/or seeking their input into decisions that affect them. As a result, many colleagues feel they 'have no voice'.[23]

2. Less time is invested in sponsorship and mentoring of employees of colour, making it harder[24] for them to access important career opportunities.

3. Employees of colour are less likely to spend time working on sought-after opportunities, which attract more recognition, due to biased resourcing decisions favouring white colleagues.

Managers

Managers play a vital role in organizations. They communicate strategic decisions; set their team's direction; recruit, motivate and manage team members; fulfil myriad HR activities; implement corporate and functional initiatives; participate in numerous business processes; manage budgets and manage upwards. All in a context where constant organizational change is the norm. And the manager role is becoming more critical, with 85% of employees[25] saying their managers will be 'more' or 'as important' in the future world of work.

What is managers' experience of our time culture? Research shows that 78% of managers report that their volume of work has increased, and 67% say its pace has become more rapid. Their contracted working hours have risen by one hour daily since 2012, adding up to 29 extra days of work each year and effectively cancelling out a typical annual leave entitlement of 20 days plus bank holidays. Furthermore, 92% of managers work longer than these contracted hours.[26] This constant time pressure inevitably has an impact on managers' wellbeing: 57% experienced insomnia, sleep loss or muscular problems in the previous three months and half experienced stress.

Yet organizations are systematically underinvesting in managers. According to a study by the consulting group BCG[27] in March 2020:

> Companies often overlook frontline leaders in their planning for leadership training and development. Most such leaders are in their first or second leadership role, advancing from 'doing' to 'leading'… They need structured support, training, and development in how to be an effective leader. Yet, while leaders at this level make up or influence 80% of a company's workforce… they often receive just 20% to 30% of the organization's attention in training.

How broken time is damaging inclusion

So we have identified how our cultural time norms are causing organizational defects that hamper our efforts to deliver our best work efficiently and healthily. Our failure to embrace more time-sensitive practices is significantly impacting people's day-to-day experiences at work and their career aspirations. Businesses serious about inclusion need to realize that until they re-evaluate the way they value and invest time at work, broad swathes of their workforces will continue to feel disadvantaged and demotivated.

Businesses aren't operating in isolation though. They are buffeted and inspired by developments in society, politics and the natural world. In Chapter 4, we will look at these wider factors influencing our relationship with time, and how they are driving greater urgency for business leaders to respond.

Chapter 4
Changing times

The factors influencing our wider relationship with time

This chapter explores:

- population demographics, living arrangements and workforce participation
- the developing impacts of the COVID-19 pandemic
- technology
- climate change and ESG
- social equality and justice
- the law
- why it's the 'how' that matters now.

BUSINESSES DON'T OPERATE in a vacuum. Whether publicly or privately owned, they are subject to wider forces and pressures to which they have to respond to in order to survive and succeed over the long term. Anticipating market trends and customers' future needs is just the tip of the iceberg. Businesses have to adapt to increasing globalization, keep up with breakneck developments in technology, figure out the impact of evolving workforce demographics and climate change on their industry, and demonstrate rock-solid ethics and integrity under the microscope of social justice campaigns and legal and regulatory requirements. Businesses are being held increasingly accountable, not just to their financial investors, but to a widening group of stakeholders and the court of public opinion. These external forces have a significant impact on how businesses are run and the way we work, including how we spend our time at work: what we attend to, what we prioritize, what we ignore (and what will bite us back). Let's take a closer look at some of these factors now.

Population demographics, living arrangements and workforce participation

Not only are there more of us than ever before, but we're living longer. The UK population is expected to surpass 69.6 million[1] by mid-2029 and by 2032 our life expectancy[2] will be 83 years for men and 87 years for women. Our population is ageing too: in 50 years' time, one in four of us will be over 65 years of age. Under-forties conception rates continue to decrease, with fertility challenges affecting one in six couples.[3] Marriage and divorce are steadily declining while cohabiting, multigenerational households and living alone are on the rise.[4] More young adults are living with their parents for longer. Dual-earner households are now the norm,[5] while just under 15% of families in the United Kingdom are single-parent families. These realities mean that the profile of our workforce is changing in several ways. First, according to the *Taylor Review of Modern Working Practices*,[6] there are more older workers with almost three in 10 workers now over 50. Second, levels of part-time employment (26%) and self-employment (15%) are rising. Third, under-employment – where people would like to work more hours than they do – persists.

All this adds up to one conclusion – that 'a number of people are not likely to be working in the way that best suits them'.[7] Consequently, people are looking elsewhere for work that meets their needs. In 2017, almost 60%[8] of permanent employees in the United Kingdom were engaging in gig economy activity (such as trading their time and skills via online platforms, providing transport or delivering goods) on top of their 'day job', while 2020/21 broke the record for the highest number of new businesses incorporated at Companies House.[9] Businesses are also pushing this trend towards self-employment, with 51%[10] expecting to grow their contingent/outsourced workforce as opposed to growing their in-house (employed) workforce.

As in other areas, the picture is more challenging for people of colour, who have an underemployment rate of 15.3% compared with 11.5% for white workers. They face the double barrier of being less likely to participate in the workforce *and* less likely to progress in their careers. People of colour and ethnic minorities make up 12.5% of the working age population, yet they comprise only 10% of the workforce, reducing to 6% at executive level.[11]

At the same time, businesses are far more aware of the value of more diverse workforces. McKinsey analysis in 2015[12] established that companies with more diverse workforces financially outperform their industry competitors, and that the converse is also true. Full representation of people of colour in the workforce would boost the UK economy by £24 billion a year, or 1.3% of GDP.[13] Gender matters too: research conducted in 2020[14] found that 'companies with greater gender diversity in leadership roles and promotions, and with more women in highly compensated and revenue-producing jobs, generate a more positive experience for all employees throughout their organizations'.

Ultimately, as the CIPD put it, 'there is a degree of mismatch between the sort of jobs people want and the sort of jobs the labour market is delivering'.[15] There's already a disconnect between the working hours and environment that people want versus what they have. Without meaningful change, this is only going to widen. During our longer working lives, more of us will be supporting older relatives and/or younger dependants, so work will need to better accommodate caring responsibilities. With more people living alone, the social connections and interactions afforded by work will be highly valued, particularly by younger employees looking to learn on the job from experienced colleagues. Taking time to listen, understand, empathize and develop other colleagues will become a first-order factor influencing people's experiences at work from day to day.

The developing impacts of the COVID-19 pandemic

Among many knowledge workers, the COVID-19 pandemic of the early 2020s will be remembered for mass-enforced remote working, even in those industries and companies where the previously unshakeable mantra had been 'it can't be done here'. The impact on employees depended on your industry, role, age, gender, ethnicity and home life. Some were placed on furlough, with the joys of unexpected paid (in the United Kingdom at least) leave tempered by the increased isolation, anxiety around job security and loss of purpose that furlough can bring. Others were hit by job losses straight away, or faced delayed or rescinded start dates. Employees in shared accommodation struggled with limited space and strained broadband; stressed parents and carers suffered the triple whammy of home schooling, childcare and work without their usual support network. Broadly, women's working hours and careers were hit harder than men's,[16] while young people, certain ethnic groups and disabled people now face greater risk of future unemployment.[17] People's mental resilience was challenged by worry, technology overload, uncertainty and confinement. Many were 'Zoomed out', yet felt disconnected from colleagues; 59% missed their office interactions and only a quarter of employees actually reported feeling more engaged with their organization during the crisis.[18]

There were some silver linings, though: some found 100% remote working preferable, and few missed their daily commute. Many valued the ability to reshape their working hours to accommodate exercise, school runs and domestic tasks. During 2020, employers' attention shifted towards providing mental health support, enhancing leave allowances and encouraging healthier work habits. One senior HR director confirmed that, for them, 'it is more important now to help employees distinguish between work and home life, how and when to stop, and the importance of breaks and lunch for productivity and wellbeing'.

Although the long-term impacts of the pandemic on the world of work remain to be seen, many industries expect to split work more evenly between home and office in future.[19] Demand from employees for all forms of flexibility is high: 87% of employees want to work flexibly[20] and, in one survey, 80% of working parents said they would prefer not to revert to their pre-COVID arrangements.[21] HR and business leaders are anticipating that people will negotiate harder for their preferred working pattern.[22] Employers are more aware of employees' home lives, and are realizing that what works for one individual doesn't necessarily work for another. The shift towards greater individualization is here.

People's views on *how* we spend our time at work are also evolving. Employees are less prepared to waste time on redundant meetings and inefficient practices, or to accept competitive, dysfunctional or exclusive behaviours. Younger employees want more time working alongside senior colleagues. Employers know this: one managing partner from a global law firm admitted[23] that their experience of the pandemic had changed their mindset, and they were now actively considering how their working practices and environment needed to adapt.

Technology

We have witnessed a breathtaking pace in technology adoption and integration in recent years, and this is expected to continue unabated and even accelerate.[24] The pandemic triggered a scramble by companies to digitize their working practices, with Microsoft CEO Satya Nadella observing at the end of April 2020 that 'we've seen 2 years' worth of digital transformation in 2 months'.[25] Since 2020, businesses have continued to invest significantly in automation, cloud computing, digital platforms and data analytics, while capabilities such as AI (artificial intelligence), encryption and robotics are increasingly being considered.[26] At the time of writing in 2021, pre-pandemic predictions that as much as one-third of workplace activities could be automated by 2030[27] looked comfortably on-target.

The impact is already being felt in organizations. Business leaders are identifying new services that offer competitive advantages, redesigning their operating models around these and transforming front and back office operations.[28] Digital tools are progressively doing more of the lower value, higher frequency work with skilled employees focusing on complex and value-added activities. In financial services organizations, these changes are already reshaping workforces, while in professional services, the impact has been greatest in audit and accounting, then technology and media consulting, with the law and executive search adapting more slowly.[29]

The impact on our work lives will be huge: by 2025, the time spent on existing work activities globally by humans and machines will be equal,[30] and 85 million jobs around the world are anticipated to be 'displaced' as a result, while 97 million new roles will emerge. Digitization has already led to the fragmentation of working time, unproductive multitasking and the phenomenon of 'time confetti' – originally described by author Brigid Schulte in *Overwhelmed: Work, Love and Play When No One Has the Time*[31] – whereby we lose millions of tiny bits of productive time. E-presenteeism and e-surveillance are on the rise, and 61% of managers say that technology has made it difficult to switch off from work.[32] Loneliness at work is spreading; in *The Lonely Century*, Noreena Hertz charts how the creep of technology is displacing time for human interaction, leading to feelings of invisibility and isolation. Research shows that 42% of us lack a close friend at work,[33] and leaders aren't immune either: in one study, half of CEOs reported experiencing loneliness in their role.[34] Loneliness doesn't just affect our emotional wellbeing, it affects our work quality too: 61% of those CEOs believed it hindered their performance and 38% of employees said it affected their productivity.

We will need to devote more time to training, developing and reskilling employees to help displaced workers find new roles and succeed in these. Better mid-career job training and on-the-job training will be essential along with shorter, more effective ways of learning. As technology makes it easier to gather data from across the workforce and wider ecosystem, taking the time to seek and listen to different perspectives and weave these into organizational improvement projects will help to nurture a collaborative and inclusive culture. In short, we need to focus on fostering humanity at work and enabling longer careers in this era of automation, big data and algorithms.

Climate change and ESG

In the 2015 Paris Agreement, 270 countries agreed to take action to limit global warming to below 2°C and ideally 1.5°C in order to avoid irreversible and catastrophic environmental consequences. Business is taking note, albeit slowly: the rise of environmental, social and governance (ESG) investing has brought sustainability concerns into investment processes and decision-making. In parallel, shareholder-focused capitalism that uses exclusively financial metrics of success is increasingly being rejected in favour of broader stakeholder capitalism, helped by research showing that good corporate sustainability performance is associated with good financial results.[35] Today, using Global Reporting Initiative standards,[36] 80% of the world's largest corporations report and are assessed on how well they manage their impact on the wider community and the environment.[37]

What's driving this adoption? There is greater pressure than ever before on businesses to consider their impact on employees, society and the environment. Today, analysts estimate that an organization's reputation is worth 20–30% of market cap across the FTSE and S&P indices.[38] Activist investors are exerting influence on boards and executives – witness the outcry surrounding mining giant Rio Tinto's desecration of Aboriginal sacred ground in Australia in 2020, followed by the ousting of its chairman, CEO and two other executives.[39] There is also greater scrutiny by the public, investors and employees of a company's words versus its actions. One example is the executive pay furore early into the pandemic, where bosses at 36 companies in the benchmark FTSE 100 index announced voluntary cuts to their salaries in sympathy with furloughed or released employees. The foregone salaries were, in many cases, comfortably offset by the stock market's bounce back a few months later where those leaders profited from improved share prices.

Faced with a sceptical and increasingly judgmental public, companies need to prioritize time spent improving and communicating their ESG performance. As influential investors push companies harder to follow through on their commitments, so employees are increasingly making their views known through protests, strikes and public campaigns against corporate decisions that run counter to stated ESG goals. Businesses have to spend more time listening to the concerns of their stakeholders and demonstrating meaningful change, not just funding annual corporate social responsibility (CSR) initiatives.

Social equality and justice

Gender bias, racial injustice, modern slavery, LGBTQ+ aggression, the increasing divide between the 'haves' and the 'have nots'... The litany of social injustices and inequalities still prevalent in our nations and society is sobering. Recent global movements such as #MeToo and Black Lives Matter have punctured public consciousness and generated a tidal wave of calls for institutions to tackle these issues. Yet McKinsey's analysis of 1000 companies over six years found that 'most [companies] have made little progress, are stalled or slipping backward'.[40] Furthermore, in a March 2020 survey, 27% of D&I leaders reported that their organizations had put all or most D&I initiatives on hold as a result of the COVID-19 pandemic[41] – it remains to be seen how many of those initiatives will be picked back up as the pandemic recedes.

Progress towards closing the gender pay gap is slow, and women are still largely excluded from the highest-paying business jobs. Encouragingly, the target to see an average of 33% of board roles across FTSE 350 companies occupied by women before the end of 2020 was achieved, but over four in 10 of those companies had failed to reach this target individually and 18 boards had only one female member. Outside of the boardroom, only 13% of FTSE 100 executive roles were held by women.

Progress in improving social mobility generally in the United Kingdom is poor to non-existent, with Sarah Atkinson, chief executive of the Social Mobility Foundation, observing that 'levelling up is at risk of becoming a cruel joke... the situation is dire'.[42] Existing social inequalities have been exacerbated by the economic downturn triggered by the pandemic. Of the 570,000 people who had lost their jobs by November 2020, the impact fell disproportionately on ethnic minorities, and younger and older workers, especially those in lower paid roles.[43]

As shocking treatment of black people by the police, especially in America, provoked riots and global condemnation, businesses came under fire for failing to tackle white privilege and the multiple entrenched barriers faced by black employees in progressing their careers. Despite the flurry of corporate statements of support for protesters, meaningful action lagged behind. After the murder of George Floyd, 75% of large US public companies called for racial justice, but just 10% mentioned action they were taking in their own organizations.[44] In the United Kingdom, there are currently no black chief executives, chief financial officers or chairs in the FTSE 100,[45] and widespread calls to introduce ethnicity pay gap reporting have not yet convinced the UK Government to implement this.[46]

LGBTQ+ inclusion (support for individuals who identify in terms of gender and/or sexuality as lesbian, gay, bisexual, transgender, queer or questioning or other) at work has advanced in recent years, with the majority of large organizations now having an active LGBTQ+ employee network, often supported by an allies' programme and a wide range of initiatives, from annual Pride marches to LGBTQ+ friendly policies. Yet 35% of LGBTQ+ employees still hide their sexual orientation at work for fear of discrimination, 18% have experienced negative behaviour at work[47] and aggression towards trans individuals in particular continues to rise in society generally.[48]

With D&I efforts now being linked directly to risk management, investment decisions and corporate stability by ratings agencies[49] and fund managers, businesses need to prioritize more time and resources for diversity and inclusion or face the financial and reputational consequences. This means taking time, across all levels and functions, to ensure that diverse employees are being listened to, are able to contribute fully and are seeing this reflected in their professional outcomes.

The law

The legislative and regulatory context in which businesses are operating today is constantly changing, dictating new rules and expectations as to how companies should manage their businesses responsibly. Let's dip briefly into some of these major reforms.

- The United Kingdom's Corporate Governance Code pushes businesses to pay greater attention to the way work gets done and to their relationships with different groups of stakeholders, and to make their workforces and management structures as diverse as possible.[50] However, Sir Jon Thompson, CEO of the Financial Reporting Council, lamented in November 2020 that 'some companies are continuing to take a formulaic approach to corporate governance driven by compliance, rather than focusing on outcomes'.

- General Data Protection Regulation (GDPR) was introduced in the United Kingdom in May 2018 to create greater transparency in the way businesses obtain, use and store people's personal data, and to protect people's right to keep this information private.[51] Business boomed for lawyers as companies rushed to publish privacy statements and disclaimers in order to comply.

- Meanwhile, in late 2019 the UK Government consulted on proposals to establish a new single enforcement body to protect people's rights at work, particularly those vulnerable to exploitation and/or in low-paid roles. Eventually, on 8 June 2021, the creation of a new 'workers' watchdog' was announced.[52]

- IR35 legislation introduced in April 2000 required organizations to reclassify certain contractors as 'employees' for tax purposes if they met certain conditions around supervision, direction and control of their work.[53]

In April 2017, this regime was replaced by the off-payroll working rules in the public sector and in April 2021, similar off-payroll working rules (commonly still referred to as IR35) were extended to the private sector requiring medium and large private sector organizations to assess carefully whether their contractors count as 'employees' for tax purposes.

- Then there are industry-specific regulations that are driving substantial changes within certain sectors. One example is the Senior Managers & Certification Regime (SMCR)[54] in the regulated financial services industry. In the wake of the last financial crisis, major frauds and governance failures, SMCR effectively holds individuals at every level more accountable for their actions and liable for prosecution in the event of misconduct.

- Following Britain's exit from the European Union, employment law, tax structures and regulatory frameworks remain broadly unchanged in the immediate term, but there are new proposals on the table for discussion. A government review of employment law is underway,[55] with rumours circulating that it will ditch the EU's Working Time Directive, which caps average weekly working hours at 48. While a Brexit trade deal was agreed at the eleventh hour, this doesn't cover services. So new regulatory frameworks and tax reform in financial services are being considered, not least to protect London's status as a global financial capital.

These reforms, together with the substantial shift in mindset triggered by the COVID-19 pandemic, will hopefully open up better quality work opportunities to more people and allow employees to more easily manage their home lives alongside their work commitments. In tandem, businesses will have to be more transparent about how work is allocated, delivered and paid for, and how they are collecting and using employee data. Finally, the aim of many of these regulatory and legal frameworks is to improve the culture in business so that more people 'do the right thing' in their day-to-day work, rather than just tick the boxes on mandatory compliance training. How we collectively spend our time at work is under greater scrutiny than ever before.

It's the 'how' that matters now

Throughout this chapter, we have seen how organizations are faced with a wide range of external pressures and influences. As they redesign floor plans and operating models for post-pandemic, highly automated office life, businesses will need to pay more attention to *how* we work in future, not just what we work on or where we do it. They will need to invest heavily in bringing sustainable decisions and behaviours firmly into the front line and devolve greater autonomy and choice over working hours and arrangements to employees. Employees will be less willing to compromise their time and more courageous in challenging their employers around work–life balance, wasted time at work, and dysfunctional or exclusive behaviours. To strengthen social glue and belonging amidst automation and virtual working, executives will need to lead with empathy and managers will need to become coaches, not supervisors.

By testing ideas and encouraging input from different employee groups and wider stakeholders, businesses will discover solutions that work better for everyone *and* benefit the bottom line. But being cautious or holding back won't cut it. In Chapter 5 we'll see why businesses need to act urgently to respond to the external influences described above and to fix our broken relationship with time.

Chapter 5
Out of time

How 'broken' time is hurting your business, and why you need to act now

This chapter explores:

- how 'broken' time is hurting productivity
- how 'broken' time is hurting diversity and inclusion
- the impact on employee engagement, motivation and retention
- how 'broken' time is damaging our wellbeing
- why this is urgent.

S O FAR, YOU may be nodding your head in recognition of the organizational issues described, and making a mental note to add these to the list of things you plan to tackle in your own organization. Perhaps you're thinking, 'We can sort out those other pressing priorities first and then crack on with addressing the time failings that are holding our business back.' If you're acknowledging the need to look afresh at your time culture, great! But kicking this systemic problem into the long grass in the mistaken belief that it's not an immediate priority is a strategy that will come back to bite you. There isn't any time to lose. We're quite simply out of time.

Our broken time culture has been hurting our businesses and the people who work in them for too long already, and the signs of damage are in plain sight. Without clear, collective action, nothing will materially change and the consequences will accumulate. Not only that, it will limit the success of other initiatives that you may be working hard to achieve – whether a reorganization, a new strategic direction, stakeholder messaging or employee wellbeing 'solutions', to name a few.

The twin challenges at the heart of fixing our time culture are that: (1) it is deeply ingrained in every aspect of our organizations; and (2) it feels hard to get your hands around it. So it is understandable that you may feel tempted to park this on the sidelines and instead introduce incremental improvements to work policies and processes. Your business hasn't failed yet because of your time culture, has it? So it's unlikely to fail now, right? Wrong. The steady drips of your time defects are eroding progress towards your business goals and will continue to do so. The unspoken 'time deal' in your organization – what employees give versus what they get in return – is not working for a large number of people. It's visible in:

- the reduced productivity despite the lengthening work week
- the homogeneity of your senior leadership cadre and your stubborn gender and ethnicity pay gaps
- the stalling retention rates as employees search for a better time deal or exit their professional careers completely
- the escalating statistics of mental and physical ill-health at work.

We're in the midst of a massive revolution in the world of work: we're designing new operating models, launching new technologies and rethinking why we need offices. But these exciting, forwarding-looking developments are being constructed on top of a foundation that needs to be fundamentally re-laid. This chapter sets out the evidence for urgent action. The time bomb is ticking loud and clear.

How 'broken' time is hurting productivity

In his 1930 essay, John Maynard Keynes predicted that by 2030 we would be enjoying highly productive work lives and working a maximum of 15 hours per week, thanks to advances in technology and efficiency.[1] Our biggest challenge would be figuring out what to do with all our leisure time. Only the 'strenuous purposeful money-makers... who blindly pursue wealth' would be working more weekly hours.

Keynes wasn't completely wrong. Productivity growth up until the 1970s was matched by increases in our leisure time, and research by the OECD confirms productivity is highest when people spend fewer hours working.[2] But when we compare Keynes' optimistic prediction with today's reality, the differences are stark. The productivity of the United Kingdom is lower than that of most other nations, after declining for decades. Our present productivity slowdown is the worst it has been for 250 years,[3] and successive governments have failed to crack this 'productivity puzzle'.

Why does productivity matter? It is generally accepted to be a key source of economic growth and competitiveness. So how do we define productivity? In economic terms, productivity is *a measure of output per unit of input*. At the level of national and global economies, one of the most widely used measures of productivity is gross domestic product (GDP) per hour worked. But what about in the context of professional roles and industries when we're not churning out widgets? A simple definition in lay terms is getting the results you want with less time and effort. Measuring productivity is more complex than simply measuring output, and approaches will vary depending on your business, function and role.

Back to our 'productivity puzzle'. Its causes are many and varied, but one contributing factor is our current mindset about time at work. Three aspects in particular are damaging our productivity at work:

1. *We accept 'overwork' as the norm.* As we have now seen, our excessively long working hours are associated with 'lower productivity, poor work performance, health problems and low employee motivation'.[4] Since the 1980s, our gains in leisure time have ceased. Quite apart from the question of the quality and purpose of life, leisure is essential for maintaining a healthy mind and body, for re-energizing ourselves, for gaining perspective on our work tasks and challenges, and for fostering creativity. Switching off from work is not only important in acknowledging the wider purpose of life, but it actually helps us be more productive when we are at work. In neurological terms, daydreaming or doing non-work activities is necessary for our brains to assimilate, store and connect information efficiently.

2. *We prize busyness over quality of work.* It's standard practice to slice and dice up the work day, pursue several strands of work at once, be pulled into meeting after meeting, and have endless 'to do' lists. The more senior your role, the more you juggle. Research by the Chartered Management Institute (CMI) found that most managers are at maximum capacity and a third are overloaded.[5] This cult of busyness sends a consistent message to people about what a productive day looks like and what it takes to succeed. In her book *Time Smart*, Ashley Whillans puts it like this: 'Employers are (mostly) rewarding the busyness cult'.[6] We're wrongly equating productivity with

busyness. Productivity should be measured in terms of what we have delivered, and whether it is good enough, not how long we have spent on it.

3. *We don't pay attention to productive working practices.* The way our organizations and work days are shaped is stifling our productivity and creativity. Bureaucratic processes and structures, an overload of competing priorities, and distractions and interruptions galore drain our time and attention, and leave many employees frustrated and neurologically depleted. In his book *Simplicity*, productivity adviser Bill Jensen explains that 'productive knowledge work is all about how we use each other's time and attention as we try to get stuff done'.[7] He argues that by failing to create an environment that allows people to concentrate, businesses are paying the price in lost creativity, innovation and competitive advantage. To take one example, 84% of businesses are poised to rapidly digitalize working processes, yet 'cognitive engineering' – creating good interactions between people and devices – is hardly mainstream in business.[8]

In redesigning the 'post-pandemic' world of work, businesses are figuring out how to stay ahead in their markets. But without dramatically changing our attitudes and habits regarding time at work, our productivity levels will continue to stagnate or worsen, and that sought-after competitive advantage will be hard to come by.

How 'broken' time is hurting diversity and inclusion

Despite diversity being a multi-billion pound industry, progress towards creating more diverse organizations is depressingly slow, and in some cases going in reverse. Executive teams remain largely homogeneous; the European Union's current gender pay gap of

14.1% has changed minimally in the past decade[9] and, among large employers in the United Kingdom, the gap has reduced by just 2% in the last four years.[10] The upwards progression of women and people of colour remains challenging across industries, while LGBTQ+ individuals continue to face additional hurdles to reaching senior levels.

What lies behind these headlines is our failure to create sufficiently inclusive environments and practices at work. Initially attracted by impressive diversity statements, policies and initiatives, once inside their new organization, 'diverse' employees too often experience a burden described as an 'emotional tax',[11] where on top of delivering in their day job they have to navigate experiences of bias, manage their own responses to these, and invest disproportionate time and effort at work in order to be valued and rewarded equally. Those who have more in common with senior leaders in terms of their demographic profile, background or home life don't carry this burden – and generally are not even aware of it.

Our cult of busyness favours task accomplishment over interpersonal curiosity, speedy shortcuts over time-consuming thoroughness and the familiar over the uncomfortable or the unknown. Consequently we're not taking enough time to:

- understand each and every employee better and appreciate their individual situations, strengths, and ambitions
- invite challenges and contributions from different perspectives
- look for data that challenges our own world views
- listen to other people's experiences and take these on board.

These habits aren't always purposeful or even conscious. Even with the best of intentions, our brains are often wired to take short-cuts that result in exclusive behaviours and an uneven playing field. In *Thinking Fast and Slow*, Daniel Kahneman explains how we go with 'WYSIATI' – 'what you see is all there is'.[12] In other words, we rush ahead with the limited data in front of us, because it's more effortful and counter-intuitive to seek out the information we don't yet have or even know we're missing – Donald Rumsfeld's famous 'unknown unknowns'[13] mentioned in Chapter 1.

The result? We're favouring the status quo, accepting partial or biased information, and going with what works for the homogeneous majority. Businesses are clinging onto a 'one size fits all' way of working that simply doesn't work for everyone. This is evident in:

- the inflexible work patterns that don't allow people the freedom to manage their own working time more productively
- the lack of diverse candidates on recruitment and promotion short-lists
- unequal access to influential networks or individuals in senior positions
- lower earnings trajectories for women (especially mothers), black and minority ethnic employees, and part-time employees
- poor retention rates at senior levels of minority demographic employees leading to significant 'stay gaps' (differing lengths of service) compared with white peers
- employment policies and benefits that favour 'majority' needs and exclude other smaller groups with different needs or circumstances.

In our high-speed, short-horizon time culture, new joiners – particularly senior hires – don't have long to establish themselves. Others are very quickly making judgements about them and their performance, and if the snap verdict isn't positive, fewer work opportunities come the new joiner's way and they are slowly marginalized. When an employee doesn't feel genuinely welcomed, valued and included, over time one of two things will tend to happen. Either they reluctantly give up the fight, accept the inevitability of the situation and fail to realize their full potential at work, or they move on in the search for a more inclusive organization that won't hold them back. Either way, the employer loses in terms of diversity, talent and performance, and the company's bottom line suffers.

The impact on employee engagement, motivation and retention

Having high levels of employee engagement is widely accepted as essential for businesses to succeed over the longer term. Some 94% of the world's most admired companies believe their competitive advantage has grown as a result of efforts to boost employee engagement.[14] Employee engagement is defined as 'a workplace approach resulting in the right conditions for all members of an organization to give of their best each day'.[15] David MacLeod OBE, co-author of the UK government's 2009 study into employee engagement and co-founder of the voluntary movement Engage for Success, told me that 'being clear what success will look like, helping people focus on the right things and giving people some ability to own things is very, very important'.

So how are we doing in the United Kingdom? Well... not great.

- Only one-third of British workers say they are engaged.
- The United Kingdom is ranked ninth for engagement levels amongst the world's twelfth largest economies.[16]
- Knowledge-based industries experience retention issues at varying levels of seniority.
- In law, many successful firms struggle to retain trainees once they've qualified.[17]
- Others see higher departure rates a few years post-qualification as parenthood or eldercare comes into play.
- Retention rates for lawyers of colour are notably lower in City firms than for white lawyers.[18]

- In consulting, attrition rates (the rate at which employees leave an organization) can reach 15 to 20%,[19] including in the Big 4 accountancies and consultancies (PwC, EY, Deloitte and KPMG).
- In financial services, one industry-wide survey found 34% of professionals were actively seeking a new job, and a whopping 86% were open to new opportunities elsewhere.[20]

The broken nature of our time culture places a heavy burden on the individual, where we have to constantly reinforce the boundaries of our own working time and keep producing the goods when we're drained of energy and inspiration. Pushing back against the system, saying we want to work in a different way, doesn't go down well unless you're the CEO.

Here's my own experience: in my late thirties I became the first employee in our large London office to request a four-day working week for a reason unrelated to childcare, eldercare or study. I wanted a better balance between my full-on (and satisfying) consulting career and other important elements of my life. My enlightened employer agreed and the new arrangement worked well enough. However, my promotions and pay rises slowed dramatically from that point onwards, so I definitely paid the price for choosing differently.

Most of us do our best within the circumstances, because we care deeply about our line of work, because we're striving towards a longer-term goal or because others depend materially on us to carry on. Yet with longer working lives a reality, it's a marathon, not a sprint. Many employees are less prepared to accept a long-hours, high-stress work culture for several decades. People are increasingly seeking a better deal around time: more flexibility over the short and long term, more time for personal and professional development, and more time in the working week to think, create and connect with colleagues in a rewarding way. Even during times of economic uncertainty, professionals are becoming more selective about who they work for and how long they stay. If you want to have committed, engaged employees, it's time to get serious about creating a better time culture.

How 'broken' time is damaging our wellbeing

Take a look at recent statistics on wellbeing at work: they paint a stark picture. Work-related stress and anxiety have been rising for the past two decades.[21] Burnout was officially recognized as an occupational phenomenon by the World Health Organization in 2019. In a 2017 study, 60–65% of British bankers aged between 25 and 44 experienced some levels of burnout,[22] while in a broader 2020 study, 75% of UK workers reported the same.[23] In the United Kingdom, work-related suicides are not officially monitored or recorded, but evidence indicates that these are increasing.[24]

Quite apart from the obvious human cost, the cost to businesses of this tsunami of ill-health is enormous. Some 17.9 million working days were lost in 2019/20 due to work-related stress, depression or anxiety.[25] Sickness absence, presenteeism and staff turnover cost employers between £33 billion and £42 billion per year.[26] And it's not just a UK problem: sleep deprivation costs US businesses more than $150 billion per annum in absences, accidents and lost productivity. The costs to our health services and to individuals are similarly heavy. Demand for UK mental health services has risen by one-third in recent years,[27] while stress and depression – even at lower levels – increase our risk of dying from a number of major causes.[28] The *Good Work* review in 2017 stated that, 'The shape and content of work and individual health and well-being are strongly related.'[29] The mindset in business is one of 'How much can we get done, and how quickly?' But humans aren't machines: we can't keep churning out results in a frenzied work culture and maintain high levels of energy and creative thinking. As Daniel Levitin says in *The organized mind*, 'If you're in a stressful environment where you're asked to produce and produce, you're unlikely to have any deep insights.'

So how does our time culture contribute to these problems? Some of the time-related factors that negatively impact our wellbeing at work are:

- work overload and time pressure
- excessively long working hours
- lack of control over how time is spent at work
- environments that are not conducive to focusing on the task at hand
- insufficient time spent connecting with colleagues
- little attention paid by organizations to employees' sleep quality or energy levels
- fragmentation of working time
- work schedules that ignore our energy peaks and troughs.

Sceptical? Take a look at your business or your own work life, and see whether you can see any of the visible evidence of these problems:

- a work day that is uniformly crammed with work activity
- people not managing to fit exercise or breaks into their day
- people only starting their own work tasks late in the day
- more people reporting feeling isolated or lonely in their roles
- work being done at weekends, on days off and during annual leave
- working late to meet deadlines
- leave entitlements not being used up
- rapid take-up of workplace counselling/GP services when offered.

If businesses truly believe people are their greatest asset, and prize innovation, quality and client service, then they need to adopt working practices that enable people to thrive. Too often we are ignoring these negative time factors and patching over them with wellbeing initiatives that do nothing to change people's day-to-day experiences of work. To reverse the decline in our wellbeing at work requires us to do two things: *acknowledge* that our time culture at work is flawed, and *collectively adopt* healthier time practices. After all, the strategy of leaving it to the individual employee to thrive against the odds is clearly not working.

Why this is urgent

Businesses are in a tight spot. On the one hand, they are facing the external pressures described in Chapter 4 and on the other, our traditional mindset and behaviours around time at work are draining energy, commitment and high performance out of our employees. How can businesses overcome these twin challenges?

To succeed, organizations will need to create:

- a time culture that fosters creativity, collaboration and resilience
- an operating model that has flexibility built into its core
- opportunities for all kinds of talented people to contribute their skills and expertise
- human-centric workplaces that foster openness, learning and empathy.

And they'll need to do it now. Why the urgency? Here are five reasons.

1. *Continued failure to meet diversity targets will bring harsher commercial consequences for businesses everywhere.* The career paths and norms that propelled current CEOs to the top appeal far less to today's ambitious employees, whose backgrounds and home lives are substantially different. Tailoring your employment practices and work culture so

everyone can flourish is imperative to the survival of a business, not a soft and fluffy 'nice to have'.

2. *Experimenting with new ways of valuing time at work will yield unforeseen advantages.* The status quo won't: as the saying goes, insanity is doing the same thing over and over and expecting different results. For economic proof, labour markets show that greater workforce flexibility brings more growth and opportunity compared with rigid, homogeneous systems. As the Confederation of British Industry (CBI) says, 'this is why flexibility matters'.[30]

3. *In a post-pandemic, virtually enabled world, businesses will be left behind by competitors who make better use of employees' time and attention.* Bill Jensen, author of *Simplicity*, declares that, 'Workplaces must organize time both so work can get done and so people can think − or you've lost your creativity, innovation, and competitive advantage, all of which reside in your workers.'

4. *Failing to look beyond your short-term, urgent goals will cost you market share and bottom line profit.* Companies with a longer-term orientation are proven to outperform their peers in earnings, revenue growth and market capitalization.[31]

5. *Gaining a head start means your business will be advantageously positioned versus competitors, and able to rebound faster when future critical events arise.* The COVID-19 pandemic proved this: firms that had already started modernizing their working practices were far less encumbered by the need to transform at speed.

Business leaders and stakeholders have also learnt that big changes can be implemented fast and very successfully: many businesses that were forced to adopt 100% remote working during 2020 actually exceeded their 2019 financial performance. There is no reason why we can't swiftly design healthier, more sustainable working practices and environments that work better for all of us.

In Part 1 we've seen the range of pressures businesses are facing today, our limiting cultural norms around time and the organizational defects that result from these. We've also acknowledged how our broken time culture prevents people from delivering their work effectively, getting on in their careers, feeling included and valued, and managing their home lives successfully alongside the demands of their work lives. Part 2 explains how businesses can value and manage time more effectively; it sets out specific practices and examples from which you can draw to plan how you might re-work time in your organization.

One-minute summary of Part I

1. Time is our most valuable asset, but our time culture at work is broken and it's hurting businesses and individuals.
2. We have social norms around time at work and we suffer from 'time blindness': we don't pay attention to *how* we spend our time at work.
3. These cause organizational 'defects' that make it harder for people to deliver their best work and flourish in their careers.
4. We need to fix the system, not the individual.
5. Collective time management is about understanding how we are all spending our time today and making conscious, strategic choices about how we want to be investing our time tomorrow.
6. Businesses need to invest time at work differently if they are serious about inclusion, improving productivity and the wellbeing of their workforce.
7. External forces have a significant impact on how we spend our time at work.
8. The nature of our organizations and work days is stifling our productivity and creativity.
9. Our advances in diversity are glacially slow, and stress, anxiety and burnout are rocketing.
10. The time bomb is ticking: businesses need to act *now*.

Part 2
Time re-worked

Better ways of valuing and
managing time

Chapter 6
Time reimagined

The six traits of time-focused organizations

This chapter explores:

- what the future of time looks like at work
- the six traits of time-focused organizations
- from traits to action.

What the future of time looks like at work

L ET'S LOOK NOW at a more effective way of collectively managing our time at work. In this chapter, we'll cover the six traits of time-focused organizations. By time-focused, I mean organizations that explicitly value working time, think about it strategically as a critical resource and reflect this in every aspect of day-to-day work.

There are two important principles to bear in mind here:

1. As we've said, this is about addressing our *systemic* time-related attitudes, habits and ways of working. It's not about mastering our to-do lists; it's about how we structure our organizations, take decisions, collaborate, manage work, lead teams and attend to interpersonal relationships.
2. The organizational goal here is to manage our *energy input* as optimally as possible to help people to show up positively and deliver their best work in a way that leaves them feeling energized and rewarded.

The six traits of time-focused organizations

So what's different about organizations that value and manage time well? Their characteristics are distilled into six traits set out below. Few organizations today are successfully living all six traits; many are making excellent progress in a number of them, while others are further behind or barely out of the starting blocks. The point of these traits is that they describe an aspirational set of outcomes to work towards; they help us to evaluate our own organizations today and they equip us to have conversations about the kind of time culture we want for the future. I appreciate that, for many people, 'organizational culture' often feels like a woolly concept and is hard to pin down in concrete terms. In Chapters 7 and 8, we'll look at a whole raft of specific practices that can help you bring these traits to life in your organization.

The six traits are:

1. *outcome obsessed:* has a laser sharp focus on outcomes and leaders role model 'time intelligence'
2. *deliberately designed:* is on a permanent quest to minimize distractions and help people focus on the important work

3. *actively aware:* fosters healthy habits and environments that enable people to do their best work

4. *career committed:* invests in long-term careers with tailored 'time deals'

5. *community cultivators:* values humanity, social cohesion and wellbeing

6. *expertly evolving:* prizes experimentation, learning and open-mindedness.

Let's take a closer look at each trait in turn.

Outcome obsessed

An *outcome obsessed* organization isn't distracted by activities and inputs; instead, it maintains an unswerving focus on its core purpose and priorities. It identifies the positive impact it wants to achieve for all stakeholders and translates these into short-, medium- and long-term business goals, striking a balance between the urgent and the important. It views collective working time as a valuable business asset that it proactively manages through the business strategy, governance and leadership approach. Businesses can apply greater rigour by quantifying an average hour's cost. 'Once hours are financially quantified, people worry more about wasting, saving or using them profitably,' confirms *The Economist.*[1] By quantifying, we're able to evaluate our collective time investments in a more data-driven way.

Time-awareness is woven into the organization's DNA, requiring a significant mindset shift. Instead of thinking about time as, 'How much can I/we get done in the short term and how quickly?', the question becomes, 'What's the most valuable way I/we can spend our time over the short, medium and longer term?' For example, if you aspire to be innovative, how much time do you spend collaborating with others? A time-focused organization collaborates with others to address industry-wide inefficiencies and create opportunities. The compression of the United Kingdom's regulatory approval process for the COVID-19 vaccines from years into weeks is a clear example of this: researchers, scientists, clinicians and regulators worked together in new ways – such as overlapping trial stages and conducting rolling data reviews – to collectively solve the monumental challenge of developing a safe and effective vaccine in record time.

An organization that factors time into decision-making is mindful of how much time it spends making decisions, and takes time to gather the best possible data. This means *not* spending more time on a decision than it is worth, knowing where ownership best sits for different decisions and seeking out different perspectives. This counters our tendency when under pressure or cognitively busy to default to stereotypes and bias, resulting in short-sighted, less inclusive decisions. It also means less likelihood of decisions being endlessly pushed around, particularly in highly matrixed organizations.

In *outcome obsessed* organizations, leaders demonstrate a deep appreciation of working time. Individually and collectively, they promote beliefs such as:

- Our time is inherently valuable.
- Thinking time is precious.
- Time spent building relationships is as valuable as time spent on tasks.
- We are all responsible for how we spend our time.
- Your time is as important as my time.
- Our time choices are interconnected.
- To make good time choices, we need open, regular communication with one another.
- Our assumptions about time may need to be reconsidered.

Leaders who are time-aware in this way reflect regularly on how they are spending their own time. Their work calendars reflect this, with time prioritized for the important stuff. Microsoft founder Bill Gates disclosed how he learnt to keep a clear diary from legendary investor Warren Buffett, saying, 'You control your time. It's not a proxy of your seriousness that you fill every minute in your schedule.'[2] With 'time intelligent' leadership, leaders model behaviours such as talking about their own time choices, asking for direct reports from those who are accountable to them and inviting continuous dialogue about the time culture by asking, 'What's working? What's not? What could work better?'

Deliberately designed

Time-focused organizations are on a permanent quest to help people focus on the important work, do this efficiently and minimize wasted time by stripping out duplication, reducing bureaucracy and streamlining processes. The corporate behemoth GE successfully embedded 'speed and simplicity' in its collective mindset and culture through its GE Workout process, which has been adopted by countless businesses.

As we debate how to shape organizations for the post-pandemic world of work, there are clear priorities emerging for making best use of the time we will spend physically together: creating solutions, developing skills and fostering social cohesion. Time-focused organizations are redesigning their operating models with these priorities squarely in mind, identifying how their new structures, processes and systems enable these outcomes, rather than obstructing them.

For example, businesses who believe that building relationships is crucial to their future success are prioritizing time and opportunities for building social bonds and trust. Those looking to boost their home-grown talent pipeline are emphasizing time spent coaching, mentoring and giving effective feedback.

Deliberate design means dealing with the distractions. Our work days tend to be highly fragmented and littered with tasks that require low levels of expertise but eat up our time. By automating or outsourcing these activities, businesses can help employees to focus on more valuable work. As Daniel Levitin explains, 'To successfully ignore distractions we have to... create systems that will encourage us to stick with the work at hand.'[3]

Organizations can also apply *deliberate design* to working hours. By moving away from Monday to Friday, 9.00 am to 5.00 pm, forward-thinking businesses are modernizing working hours, removing the bonds of a set start and finish time and allowing greater freedom underpinned by a few clearly articulated principles. These share three common features: they talk about core hours; they are based on trust with reduced controls; and they encourage undisturbed time.

With core hours, employees are expected to be available for certain parts of the day – for example, 10.00 am to 12 noon and 1.30 pm to 3.30 pm – but outside of core hours they are free to adapt their working day to suit their energy levels, personal lives and working styles.

This trust-based approach borrows a key principle from manufacturing about spans and controls. Big time spans that are lightly managed succeed in creating space for more productive, creative, time-efficient working. Conversely, short time spans that are tightly controlled actually achieve the opposite, because the control process itself takes up too much time and effort. Opening up and lightly managing the working week is more effective than rigidly controlling working hours.

By explicitly sanctioning undisturbed time, employers are encouraging employees to concentrate, do deep thinking and emerge less neuro-depleted afterwards. The Pareto Principle, also known as the 80/20 rule, posits that 80% of consequences come from 20% of the causes. Applied to work, it follows that 80% of results come from 20% of our total work effort. Time-focused organizations allow people to get that important 20% done, and done well. As Cal Newport says in his book *Deep Work*, 'three to four hours of continuous, undisturbed deep work each day is all it takes to see a transformational change in our productivity and our lives'.[4]

With *deliberate design*, work is resourced and managed transparently. Rather than scoping the task in terms of hours required, time-focused organizations are specifying the output that is required and by when, and resourcing it on that basis. This permits the employer to tap into a wider talent pool and gives employees additional opportunities to broaden or deepen their skills. How work gets resourced has a fundamental impact on diversity and inclusion, and people's career progression. Time-focused organizations take a forensic approach to resourcing decisions and look at the data to identify where certain employees are repeatedly under-resourced or overlooked for career-enhancing opportunities because they are less able to meet the time requirements or constraints specified.

When it comes to business technology, we can select tools and data that better support the ways people think, speak, and make decisions. Time-focused employers choose cognitively engineered technology that takes into account how people receive and process information, reduces the cognitive burden and creates a more positive user experience. By thoughtfully changing the default settings of our everyday tools and technologies, they build in 'nudges' that help people to adopt healthier, more productive habits.

Actively aware

The first two traits deal with fairly concrete organizational aspects: strategy, governance, processes, structure and systems. These are things that you can draw on paper and label. They will have a certain impact, but for meaningful results, the nature of everyday interactions, behaviours and informal working practices needs to change. *Actively aware* time-focused organizations tackle this head on by:

- designing environments that free up time and space for people to do their best work
- giving people as much autonomy and control over their working lives as possible
- encouraging time awareness at organizational, team and individual levels.

For people to do their best work, their environment needs to work for them. In physical terms, this means informal areas where people can catch up, pick each other's brains and socialize, and collaborative spaces for meetings, brainstorms, confidential discussions and co-creating. People can crack on with deadlines, do deep thinking and work undisturbed in quiet zones, while dedicated wellbeing areas help people to decompress, deal with difficult emotions, rest and even exercise. In tech companies where work such as coding requires long periods of intense concentration, it is standard practice to issue noise-cancelling headphones and a red indicator light to every employee. When both are on, others understand that the user is not to be disturbed. It's a low-cost and effective strategy.

The physical principles translate to the virtual environment too. Technology can be used to facilitate informal interactions through instant messaging, virtual 'drop-ins' and dedicated social time online. Collaboration tools and channels such as intranets, workflow tools, shared diaries and knowledge bases help people to locate and exchange information easily and connect with others in a timely way. Importantly, employees are able – and encouraged – to switch all of these off for extended periods during the working day in order to concentrate or to take a break.

Organizations that genuinely value collective working time give employees as much autonomy and control over their working hours as possible. This allows people to organize their time to fit with their peak energy levels, preferred working styles, personal commitments and wellbeing. To make this work requires trust and dialogue.

First, trust. For the employer/manager, this means letting go of micro-managing and monitoring, being skilled at managing remotely and measuring performance by what people have achieved, not the time they've put in. For the employee, it means being accountable for delivering agreed outputs, communicating regularly about their work status and availability, and being flexible when they are genuinely needed.

Now dialogue. Giving employees more autonomy and control doesn't mean loosening the reins and hoping for the best. It means talking and listening to people regularly about their working time and knowing where the time pain points are for different groups and individuals — for example the recent joiner who's feeling isolated; the new parent who's sleep-deprived; the team that's struggling with priority-overload; and the promising future leader who's lacking face-time with senior colleagues.

We've seen how leaders can model time-intelligent behaviours, but the onus isn't just on them. We're all responsible to a certain degree for our behaviours and choices regarding how we spend our time at work. We can blame our unproductive day on email overload, but how disciplined are we at switching our email off to concentrate on the task at hand? How often do we get our comments to a colleague at the last possible minute without thinking of the impact on their working time? Time-focused organizations encourage healthy, transparent norms around working time. In practice, this means:

- *Leaders* set the example, invite dialogue, coach others, pick up on unhelpful behaviours and hold people accountable.
- *Teams* agree the working arrangements that will help them to thrive and meet their goals. This means agreeing things such as when they will physically be together; how they will cover colleagues' non-working time and absences;

and how they will buddy up, delegate or shadow one another to work efficiently and optimize learning time.

- *Individuals* manage the boundaries of their working time; communicate clearly about their availability and progress; check their assumptions about time urgency; and are open, without apologizing, about their time constraints. And yes, sometimes this requires courage.

Career committed

This trait is about how organizations recruit, manage, develop and reward people. First, time-focused organizations are investing in longer-term relationships with employees. This is partly a consequence of the eco-system mindset that businesses are increasingly adopting, whereby relationships outside of the business are highly valued. Tellingly, 40% of global CEOs expect most of their future innovation to be co-developed with partners outside their organization.[5] Today's employee may be tomorrow's new business opportunity, and tomorrow's leader may be today's school leaver participating in your outreach programme. So it pays to think beyond the timespan of the employment contract.

Businesses are investing more time in nurturing careers even before people have started out in the world of work or officially joined as an employee, knowing that this helps to raise the profile of their industry across more diverse demographics and broaden the talent pool over time. Working with schools, apprenticeships, cross-industry campaigns and skills-building programmes provides some examples of this. Witness, for example, the #10000BlackInterns initiative offering 10,000 internships over five years, across 24 sectors and more than 700 companies, to help young people of colour to kickstart their careers.[6]

Once through the door, the organization takes a pragmatic, longer-term view of employees' careers, appreciating that these may need to follow different stages, pathways and timelines. They understand that it is only by providing opportunities to accelerate, pause or switch career tracks to suit the individual that they will succeed in creating a genuinely diverse workforce. They listen to people's priorities and ambitions, and encourage them to have a shot at these, knowing this might ultimately benefit the business just as much as the individual. They mirror this attitude in their organizational learning strategies, giving employees more time for professional and self-development, investing in transferable skills and promoting lifelong learning. They also excel at maintaining relationships with alumni employees, recognizing the value of a flourishing network where former employees become future clients, advocates or suppliers.

Second, organizations are transparently setting out the *time deal* on offer. This is the 'give and take' that articulates, on the one hand, what the employer is expecting in terms of working time, how this will be spent and what demands and commitments are being asked of the individual; and on the other hand, what the employee can expect in return in terms of time flexibility, rewards in the short and longer term (financial and career-related) and what support they will receive to work in a healthy, productive way.

Time-focused organizations are moving away from homogeneous time deals and tailoring these much more to the individual. This approach is reflected in workplace policies and benefits that provide people with much greater autonomy and choice within a broadly defined offer. Businesses are also recognizing the value of time-centric benefits and how these boost employee retention and commitment. The time deal informs the performance management, promotion and reward systems that rely less on heavily time-based criteria and adopt fairer, more outcome-based approaches.

For example, how often are older, male candidates who are not primary carers favoured in promotion decisions above colleagues who have to preserve time for caring responsibilities, because they are seen as being more available and less constrained by their home lives? Or how often are white colleagues promoted earlier than colleagues of colour who have to achieve far more in the same working hours in order to overcome unconsciously biased mindsets and practices? Time-focused organizations are working to reduce time bias in their people-management decisions and to ensure that people with different working patterns, career histories and backgrounds aren't being inequitably treated.

Community cultivators

For many of us, the COVID-19 pandemic reminded us sharply of our need to connect at a human level. Lately undervalued in corporate workplaces amidst the frenzy of multitasking, deadlines, travel schedules and long hours, time spent getting to know one another better and building bonds of trust drained away. Important interactions required a work output and a calendar invitation. But, as the rise of loneliness and mental ill-health in the workplace underline, we are social beings, not machines. We all have a fundamental need to feel heard, understood, included and appreciated. This can feel more challenging for under-represented groups such as LGBTQ+ individuals, people of colour, people with disabilities and neurodivergent people.

A time-focused organization places high priority on valuing individuals, fostering connectedness and linking time to wellbeing. Great managers don't just manage the work and the numbers; in time-focused organizations, managers are selected for their people skills and emotional intelligence. They listen well, include everyone, value different perspectives and demonstrate empathy. When managers aren't committed to valuing individuals, employees are twice as likely to feel excluded and nearly three times more likely to leave.[7] Furthermore, wellbeing increases when people rate their relationship with their employer highly. Nearly two-thirds of managers (62%)

say their line management relationship has a positive impact on their wellbeing.[8] Similarly, managers experience significantly less stress when they have a good relationship with their employees and vice versa.[9]

How do we foster connectedness in organizations? Neuroscience, and the science of happiness can enlighten us here. Thanks to research in these fields, we have learnt that our brains don't process time well; they work better with stories, and hold on to specific memories. And our sense of happiness is determined by our *average* happiness over time, not the *sum* of all happy moments. This doesn't mean that, to inelegantly paraphrase George Orwell,[10] all times are equal. Some times are more equal than others. In *Thinking Fast and Slow*, celebrated psychologist Daniel Kahneman explains how 'peaks and ends matter, duration does not'.[11]

Organizations that invest time in social connectedness encourage people to interact outside of work tasks and are attentive to ending work chapters and relationships well. They cultivate and reward kindness and understand that it's the organizational memories we create that knit us together into communities. Ask anyone for their best work-related memories and they'll likely tell you about a kindness remembered, a team celebration or a favourite workplace tradition. Time-focused organizations cultivate these significant events and behaviours that people will remember in the future. For example, in one organization a handbell is rung to mark an individual's or team's success, inviting others to join in the celebrations. In another, a day spent helping a chosen charity is welcomed as a reward for achieving a stretch goal. My favourite work memory? A team 'BAFTA' dinner where every team member received an award – often hilarious – for their qualities that colleagues most appreciated.

Time-focused organizations make explicit the link between how we spend our working time and our wellbeing. 'At its most fundamental, work is an energy transaction,' observed anthropologist and author James Suzman.[12] Healthy working is about managing our energy. We're humans, not machines, so we need to minimize energy depletion, restore energy levels and keep our minds and bodies healthy. The *Good Work* review concludes by saying that 'the shape and content of work and individual health and well-being are strongly related. For the benefit for firms, workers and the public interest, we need to develop a more proactive approach to workplace health.'[13]

Proactive organizations are doing more than offering gym access, medical benefits, resilience training and mindfulness sessions. They are investing time in promoting healthy work habits that increase our time affluence and wellbeing. For example, one HR leader coaches her team on healthy time habits: 'I talk to my team about how to chunk up their time, don't do emails constantly throughout the day. And we're always talking about blocking out time in your calendar that's just "you" time.' If someone is stressed, she encourages them to skip the meeting and go for a walk, saying, 'We'll have a much better conversation afterwards.'

Expertly evolving

The final trait of time-focused organizations describes their attitude towards the future. They recognize that the outside world – society, their industry, their markets and customers – is constantly changing, and so too are the needs of their workforce. They appreciate that however efficient, productive and healthy it is, the way we work today may not be the right way to work tomorrow. Investing in improving their time culture may yield a positive impact in the short term, but if they tick the box to say 'done', this isn't going to position them for continued success over the longer term.

This is easier said than done, of course. Employees everywhere are tired of corporate initiatives, branded change programmes and the latest round of 'moving the deckchairs'. Loss-aversion is a natural human trait, meaning we are biased towards maintaining the status quo. And confidence in our employer's ability to manage change is low: fewer than one-third of managers believe that senior managers are able to manage change well.[14] To expertly evolve, organizations have to help their employees adopt a psychological mindset where they embrace change willingly and believe they can develop new skills and work in new ways. By adopting a 'growth' rather than 'fixed' mindset, as described by Carol Dweck, professor at Stanford University and a leading voice in mindset psychology, organizations can foster the skills, curiosity and resilience needed to continuously adapt. They achieve this through experimenting and learning, keeping a collectively open mind, encouraging resourcefulness through coaching practices and building longer-term time-management capability.

'Over the long run, superior performance depends on superior learning.' In his classic article 'Building Learning Organizations', management guru Peter Senge describes how businesses that are successful over the longer term invest a huge proportion of their time in continuous learning.[15] Leaders 'help people... to see beyond the superficial conditions and events into the underlying causes of problems'; in turn, people 'are continually expanding their capabilities to shape their future'.

In an *expertly evolving* organization, people regularly switch between two modes: experimenting and reflecting. Experimenting happens through questioning, testing, trialling and piloting, *and* rewarding all of these activities. It requires a safe environment for people to take measured risks and for failure to be accepted as a necessary part of learning and growing. Reflecting happens through feedback, reviews and data-driven assessments. By stepping away from the detail to the bird's eye view, people can look more holistically at the situation, and are better able to spot underlying factors and grow their own capabilities.

How often have you or a colleague suggested an idea that might solve a thorny problem or result in an innovation, only for it to be instantly discounted or slide quietly off the agenda? Keeping a collectively open mind is a learned skill that takes conscious, repeated effort. We've seen how decisions tend to be made on the basis of 'WYSIATI' (what you see is all there is) – that is, we prefer to make quick decisions based on the limited information in front of us. Not only do we exclude hard-to-gather data, but we tend to conform to 'group-think' when generating ideas and making decisions. Group-think has led to major business disasters and appalling social scandals, as Margaret Heffernan explains in her book *Wilful Blindness*,[16] but it feels extremely uncomfortable being the one dissenting voice amidst a chorus of agreement.

Expertly evolving organizations work hard to counter these behavioural traps. They prize openness to new information, even if that involves updating assumptions or re-working plans. In meetings, they ask 'What don't we know yet?' and ensure that everyone contributes their views before a decision is made. In analyses, they look for the data that doesn't fit the pattern and in brainstorming, they are attentive to the smallest or most unlikely-sounding ideas from unexpected sources. They encourage employees to pursue outside interests and collaborations, knowing that these will help to bring in lateral thinking from other fields.

In this environment, the role of the manager changes from supervisor to leader. A supervisor tends to micro-manage the team's work, review it and correct it, and is frequently called upon to make a multitude of decisions. They retain a high level of control over the team's work. In contrast, when acting as a leader, the manager becomes coach and facilitator. Rather than being the expert who provides the answers, the manager uses coaching techniques to encourage team members to explore possibilities, try different strategies and reflect on their successes and failures.

Collective time management is like a muscle: without regular training, it will weaken in the face of ever-changing priorities, pressures and new strategic initiatives. To complement the informal day-to-day coaching by managers, *expertly evolving* organizations maintain strong organizational muscles by building awareness and skills in collective time management through dedicated workshops and training sessions.

From traits to action

We've taken a first look at these six traits of time-focused organizations. They drive improved retention, creativity, diversity, belonging, wellbeing and ownership, and in terms of business outcomes, contribute to greater business resilience, productivity, agility and innovation. Adopting these traits will help you to make progress in other organizational goals as well as improving your time culture. In the following chapters, we'll cover tangible time solutions that you can consider for your own organization as we switch into practical mode.

Chapter 7
Time solutions

The positive time practices that enable organizations to flourish

This chapter explores:

- *outcome obsessed* organizations
- *deliberately designed* organizations
- *actively aware* organizations
- shifting from the organization to the individual.

WHAT EXACTLY DOES good collective time management at work look like? How can we spot it in action or describe it to colleagues? While the six traits discussed in Chapter 6 describe the *broad characteristics* of time-focused organizations, this chapter and Chapter 8 describe the positive practices – *specific actions* – that, when spread and sustained across the business, add up to a significant shift in organizational behaviour and outcomes. All twenty-four time solutions described in this book are listed in Appendix 3. They won't all necessarily apply to your business: this will depend on the nature of your current time practices, defects and organizational set-up. If you are wondering how to identify the most important ones to implement or the order in which to tackle these, then hold that thought. Part 3 will guide you through the whole implementation approach from assessment and diagnosis to phasing and pacing, from building momentum to sustaining your new practices.

Outcome obsessed organizations

A more strategic mindset and approach to managing time require a laser-sharp focus on outcomes and the positive impact you want to achieve, not just for your clients and shareholders but also for your employees and other stakeholders.

#1 *Agree your strategic time investments*

As a leadership team, ask yourselves, 'How do we collectively want to invest our time in this organization?' and include your time priorities and investments for the short, medium and long term in your strategic plan. There'll be some tough decisions involved: as a wise colleague once reminded me, 'You don't have a strategy until you know what you're *not* doing.' Once you've identified your time priorities, how will you know whether you are sticking to these? By holding regular standback sessions – say every six months – at which you ask yourselves: 'Are we still spending our time on the right things?' Bring in relevant data to make this as objective an evaluation as possible; this is your chance to review your time investments from a bird's eye view and respond to any changes in your operating context.

A laser-sharp focus on outcomes also applies to how you fulfil your reporting requirements. In November 2020, the Financial Reporting Council's CEO, Sir Jon Thompson, remarked, 'It's clear that some companies are continuing to take a formulaic approach to corporate governance driven by compliance rather than focusing on outcomes, supported by high quality and transparent evidence.'[1] Beware the annual report presented as a polished hive of activity designed to tick many boxes and instead clearly set out your target outcomes and the evidence of your progress towards these.

If you're a publicly owned company, you can take the bold step to stop issuing quarterly earnings estimates: these drive attention towards short-term financial targets and quick fixes to boost the share price. It is hardly a recipe for a sustainable business model. If you're not convinced, the findings of an analysis of 615 US public companies may sway you: these provided solid evidence that companies with a 'long-term orientation' outperformed their peers across a range of financial and operational measures.[2]

#2 Define what you mean by 'productive'

When productivity is not clearly defined, people don't know whether they're spending their time on the important stuff, so spell out what a productive day or week looks like. Back this up with a few well-chosen metrics: the key here is to focus on outcomes, not milestones or inputs. For example, the successful adoption of a new product, not the launch, and definitely *not* the hours spent online by remote workers. Leaders can use their informal radar to monitor productivity, inclusion and wellbeing by asking: 'What are we seeing and hearing? What new patterns are we spotting?' For example, in 2020 a leading property firm compared productivity in its Asia offices during 100% remote working, a partial return to the office and 100% office-based working. They discovered that productivity was lowest when people were split between home and the office; this has guided their design of a more productive hybrid-working model in future.

In organizations that are highly focused and productive, leaders and their teams know the value of their time. This can be quantified in relatively simple terms: if you're in a role where you charge out your time to clients, it's typically your full hourly fee rate. For other roles and areas, HR can calculate the average revenue per employee, per office, per hour (using revenue as a proxy for value added). You can then use your hourly time value to calculate and monitor your collective investment of time on different activities. For example, some consulting firms apply P&Ls to individual projects, including the time invested in winning the work. This provides robust data for identifying the more attractive opportunities and deciding not to pursue others.

With any measurement activity, there is always a risk of getting lost in the numbers and losing sight of the driving purpose behind what you're measuring. To counteract this, define the desired outcomes for major work activities with input from clients and partners. What will success look like? What will people do, say or know that is different from now? For example, the successful outcome of e-learning isn't completing the roll-out on time with excellent participation rates; it's when you can observe, with evidence, the new skills being put to use confidently.

#3 Build diversity into decision-making

Before you can build diversity into your decision-making, a prerequisite is to have specified clearly who makes which decisions and who is answerable for what. Accountability expert Dr Brian Dive defines accountability as 'being answerable to another person for a product, process, or result that is measurable in terms of quantity, quality, and time'.[3] But as many of us have no doubt experienced, accountability can often be bafflingly opaque. If there's no name(s), it isn't clear, and when it isn't clear, decisions drain unnecessary time.

Good quality decision-making (outside of a crisis) requires time to invite wider views, and to discuss and debate. At board level, this requires a diverse mix of skills, thought, experience and backgrounds across board members. If your board isn't as diverse yet as you'd like, a good way to gain different views and test proposals is to set up a mirror board. This is a shadow board where participants are drawn from across the organization – either from the pipeline of future leaders or according to specific criteria. For example, a global insurance firm appointed a mirror board comprising a younger, more diverse group of employees to view the executive team's papers and contribute to their debate. Mirror boarding has the added benefit of developing colleagues and giving them valuable insight into strategic considerations.

When we are preparing to make decisions, we often fall into the trap of over-investing in crafting the arguments, proposal and papers, and under-investing in having a rich and full debate. By shortening the pre-reading for meetings, particularly at board and executive levels, we can invest our time instead in a more holistic, diverse discussion, asking questions such as, 'Which of these investments will drive client outcomes? Which is best for employees?' This may feel uncomfortably different: as one FTSE 100 Board member wryly commented to me, 'diversity in the boardroom means decisions take longer and it's messier. Group think is easier!'… with the unspoken agreement here that group think is still to be avoided at all costs.

Another effective way to mitigate against group-think is to conduct pre-mortems. This is where you invest time in imagining everything that could possibly go wrong *before* you make major decisions. Taking the time to do this before you land a decision legitimizes any lurking doubts that people may have, and encourages people to voice these. It also reduces overconfidence, fires the imagination and helps you spot hidden threats. It's a potent way to harness diversity of thought and experience.

Decision-making aside, what does leadership look like in *outcome obsessed* organizations? It is generally accepted that successful leaders are characterized by high IQ (Intelligence Quotient) and high EQ (Emotional Intelligence, or the ability to express your own emotions and understand those of other people). Leading a time-focused organization also requires TQ (Time Intelligence).

#4 Develop time-intelligent leadership practices

This starts with being open about your own time choices and letting others know how you manage your own time to maintain healthy work habits. You might explain why you've declined the invitation to an early work call or deliberately kept your camera on after a mid-morning run, while still pink and sweaty. One US executive has virtual 'walking' meetings with his team, signalling that it's good to be outside during the day without waiting until the evening. Executive coach Matt Nixon says those who cope best with the intense demands of leadership put their individual needs first, starting with the most basic of human needs: sleep. His first question to leaders is always, 'How are you sleeping?' Why? 'If you're not meeting your physical, mental health and sleep needs, everything else will be compromised.'

Modelling time-intelligent leadership also means acknowledging the impact of your time choices – including your digital habits – on others. Time-aware leaders ask other people, 'How can I help you make best use of your time? What can I do to help free up your time?' While they might work anti-social hours, they make this a private choice. For example, a consulting leader who finds evenings a productive time to work never sends emails after 9.00 pm and switches off her VPN so she's not visible online.

Time-intelligent leadership also means investing time in developing emotional intelligence in others. A number of studies have shown that emotions play a critical role in forming effective groups and achieving shared goals.[4] Time-aware leaders take time to acknowledge and discuss emotions at work; they spot emotional contagion – when a mood spreads rapidly across an organization, even virtually; and coach colleagues in processing big emotions.

Deliberately designed organizations

The goal here is to modify the organizational set-up so the structure, working patterns, resourcing and technology all align to liberate, rather than consume, working time and to give individuals greater flexibility in how and when they work.

#5 Simplify, simplify, simplify

How many levels and layers are there in your organization's hierarchy? These generally increase in complexity over time. There are different approaches to designing optimum structures; Elliott Jacques, social scientist and organizational development expert, advocated determining levels according to the *time it takes someone at each level to deliver what is needed.*[5] If you have too many layers, time and energy are wasted by people sorting out their boundaries and micromanaging unnecessarily.

Simplifying may mean pooling expertise where this makes sense. When certain work requires specialist skills and has variable demand, it is more time-efficient to centralize those skilled resources into a single team or centre of expertise. Bear in mind, though, that this will only work if the role doesn't require proximity to external customers to operate successfully. Time-focused organizations also favour decentralized operating models, giving teams greater responsibility for local decision-making and operational improvements. Being trusted to self-manage brings out the inherent creativity of teams and boosts employee engagement, which in turn boosts productivity[6] and wellbeing.

Just as organization structures acquire extra levels over time, so they also bulk out as new teams, units and departments get added. One way to counteract this is to favour temporary rather than permanent structures. When you're launching a new initiative, bring people with the required skills together into a temporary team; then on completion, task them with closing the team down and handing over to 'business as usual'. When these endings are delayed or ignored, permanent hulks are left behind in the organization structure, adding unnecessary complexity. Why not hold an organizational spring clean every year to take stock of your current operating model?

#6 Establish principles for working patterns

A hot topic today is how to define collective working hours and patterns in this new world of remote working and global talent sourcing. Many businesses are moving away from specifying formal business hours as traditional models of work are disappearing. One FTSE 250 insurance company has boldly dispensed with contracted hours and has told employees to work 'whenever and wherever you want'. This approach takes some careful management and monitoring: some employees end up working all the time and not taking enough holiday.

Instead of fixed office hours, time-focused organizations are introducing principles guiding working time, then giving people the freedom to determine the best solutions within these parameters. In an international property group, business units agreed blocks of core working hours. Where teams span time zones, the lunch hour is kept meeting-free. In other teams, working patterns are agreed on an individual basis. 2020's COVID-19 pandemic accelerated the move by many organizations towards offering 100% informal flexibility without the need for manager permission. For example, the pharmaceutical giant Novartis's 'Choice with Responsibility' programme switched from 'manager approved' to 'manager informed', allowing employees to choose their working hours provided they coordinated with colleagues and informed their manager.[7] Of course, not every employee can enjoy total freedom to decide when, where and how they work, but the point here is that all possible options are discussed openly, and a balance is struck between business and individual needs.

Increasingly, organizations in both the public and private sectors are coming around to the view that fewer rather than more working hours is beneficial to productivity.[8] In *Shorter*, Alex Soojung-Kim Pang sets out a comprehensive guide to adopting the four-day week with an argument that's hard to ignore.[9] It requires a balance between autonomy and discipline: in order to enjoy our individual time freedoms as employees (i.e. our shorter work days/weeks), we all have to stick to the rules or norms that we've agreed together, so cooperation and a strong culture are necessary. It's also essential to involve clients in redesigning your working time. If a four-day week or six-hour day sounds impossible to contemplate, why not experiment with 'summer hours' during July and August? Consulting firm PwC is adopting this concept.[10]

#7 Adopt a more time-aware approach to resourcing work

An unpredictable environment requires businesses to quickly deploy people with the right skills to where they are most needed, while the rise of technology and automation means businesses are steering their talent towards higher impact work. How work is allocated lies at the heart of inclusion as well as the commercial model: resourcing decisions have a huge impact on people's career and pay progression, and when unconscious bias isn't checked, certain employees are advantaged or disadvantaged. *Deliberately designed* organizations are shifting away from resourcing methods that rely heavily on time as an input, and thinking differently about how they match people and skills fairly to work.

With external sourcing, employers are increasingly buying solutions instead of time. Rather than specify the number of hours' or days' work required, they'll specify the task and select a suitably skilled resource who can deliver that at an acceptable cost by the deadline. Applied internally, this approach gives employees greater flexibility in how and when the work gets done and the employer gains by diversifying the pool of potential candidates.

Employers are also looking to address bias in resourcing decisions. By taking the time to review resourcing decisions through a diversity lens, challenge habits and spot resourcing patterns, organizations can make the most of their diverse workforce *and* ensure greater fairness. In management consulting, many consultancies appoint dedicated resourcing managers to handle resourcing decisions. They are senior enough to negotiate with senior sellers and adept at maintaining the detailed picture of individuals' availability, expertise and ambitions.

Time-aware resourcing isn't just about the day-to-day decisions, but about looking further ahead to project future resourcing needs. Given your business strategy and diversity goals, what skills and experience will you need to draw on? How does this compare with the expertise and people you have now? By predicting your resourcing supply and demand, you will be able to spot the future gaps you'll need to fill.

#8 Harness technology thoughtfully to free up time and boost performance

Technology has proliferated in the workplace, but our work habits haven't evolved as quickly. We're drowning in emails, stuck on conference calls all day long and can't put our fingers quickly on the data we need. But we can design and use technology in better ways that reap benefits for individuals, teams and the organization as a whole.

Forward-thinking organizations are cleaning up their data and integrating their systems. They're creating user-friendly dashboards of live, accurate data to empower managers and link their decisions directly to the business outcomes. The adoption of self-service tools – for HR, compliance, reporting and routine administration – enables businesses to cut support function costs in the short term. At first glance, this seems an obvious win and self-service tools can definitely help improve time efficiency. But if everyone is spending half a day every week (or more) on self-service activities, what is that time costing you over the longer term? Are you really getting the best value from your talented employees? Harnessing technology thoughtfully here means calculating the long-term cost/benefit of self-service tools and making sure your self-service approach adds genuine value.

Hovering near the top of many people's technology bugbear list is email overload. Employees on average receive 121 emails per day at work; some receive over 200.[11] We spend up to one-third of our time reading, answering and filing emails![12] Solutions abound: switching email servers off overnight, using work collaboration tools instead; banning cc-ing and weekend emails; and auto-deleting emails sent during annual leave. Whatever option you choose, it's time for us all to get a grip on our email culture.

#9 Nudge users into better digital choices

Deliberately designed organizations are adding features into software and tools that help people interact with them in a healthier way. Some companies have pre-designed meeting options so organizers can instantly choose between a 10 minute 'check in', a stand-up meeting or a longer one-to-one or group call. One global consultancy has pre-configured meeting options to 25 minutes or 50 minutes to give people five or 10 minutes to take a break or prepare for their next call, recognizing that attention-switching is metabolically costly and being glued to our desks and screens for long stretches is damaging to our mental and physical wellbeing.

Shifting to more virtual ways of working has given employers greater opportunity to collect and mine 'big data'. People analytics is a fast-growing field of HR where the employer collects and analyses data about employees' online habits, as well as demographics and career data. At the macro level, understanding how people spend their time at work can help you spot potential issues and trends early, including some useful indicators about your time culture and how this may be impacting people's wellbeing. For example, the data might flag up to you that a normally engaged team member has been withdrawing from online interactions, or that someone's unsustainably long or intense working hours are putting them at risk of burnout. However, this kind of big data verges on 'big brother' territory, so an ethical, transparent approach is essential

– trust between employer and employees will be damaged if people feel like they're working in a surveillance state.

Actively aware organizations

Changing an organization's culture can be incredibly hard; the most carefully designed interventions don't always succeed in changing people's behaviour. It takes a holistic, sustained effort to change what is seen as 'the norm' and to make the new norm stick. In Chapter 6, we learnt that to create a time-aware culture, organizations need to design environments that help people work productively, give them as much autonomy and control as possible, and foster greater time awareness. Here are some practical solutions to achieve this.

#10 Promote healthy habits as an essential element of productive working

There needs to be some common ground established upfront about the way of working to which you collectively aspire; this should be collaboratively developed, and cover questions such as what's important to enable a productive and healthy work mode, what support is available, and how people can encourage and constructively challenge others. Some organizations are setting out these guidelines in an organizational charter; these conversations and commitments are also happening across industries. For example, a cross-industry initiative called the Mindful Business Charter[13] has been signed by over 50 financial services, law and consumer goods companies committed to improving productivity by fostering better practices for mental health and wellbeing. Signing a charter is a public way of signalling your positive intentions as an organization; the risk, however, is that the proclamation isn't followed through with meaningful changes to workplace norms and behaviours, or discussed with clients to secure their active support.

Some of these changes relate to how downtime is viewed. We saw in the last chapter how time-aware organizations provide spaces where employees can nap, de-stress or take mental breaks. Once the preserve of trendy tech companies in Silicon Valley, these are now being taken seriously by businesses across a range of industries. Offering these spaces is one thing, but making it acceptable to be seen in them is another: how often are senior leaders spotted using these spaces, for example? They'll only get used if you explicitly and repeatedly emphasize that downtime is valued as a way of 'working at your best'. And to avoid these spaces being perceived as a way of persuading people to stay onsite for longer hours, leaders and managers still need to encourage people – through words and their own example – to leave the office at a reasonable time.

These physical spaces can be replicated in the virtual office too. Business leaders can help their teams to create space during the working day for cognitively recharging, chatting with colleagues and getting exercise. Ways of doing this include organizing informal channels for conversations and establishing 'no-fly zones' where people are encouraged to switch off from their devices or work undisturbed. One senior leader in consulting sends a recurring daily calendar invitation to everyone in her business unit to keep the lunch hour meeting-free; people are not expected to be available during this time.

#11 Re-contract differently with people about how they fulfil their roles

On giving employees more autonomy and control, the Head of Total Rewards at a global consumer products company said, 'Personally I don't care what time people do their work, as long as we can still contact each other and work as a team to deliver what we need to deliver.' Mass remote working during the pandemic of the early 2020s proved people can be trusted to work as productively at home as in the office; it also required leaders to re-evaluate how they invested their own time. For example, an

HR director in a leading property firm said, 'We are spending considerably more time preparing and sharing information from leaders to offices, from one team to another.' Leaders are thinking harder about what employees really need to understand in order to do their jobs remotely, and are giving people the information they need to make sound decisions without the safety net of a manager sitting a desk or two away.

Actively aware organizations invite people to propose how they will deliver their job responsibilities in a way that works for them *and* meets the needs of the business. Rather than a one-way, one-size-fits-all directive, they are open to creating negotiated, individualized agreements between employer and employee. For example, a part-time senior finance manager was concerned about stepping up to become financial director. Her HR leader's advice? 'Forget about time and just ask yourself whether you are up for this role. If yes, then you need to contract with the business about when you're available for work and when you're not. We can't work with you unless you're clear with us.' Of course, it's easier to craft your own role and set out your terms when you're in a senior role. But people earlier in their careers are adopting a proactive stance and being courageous in speaking up about their working hours. They are less willing to compromise this with unnecessary meetings or dysfunctional working patterns. There are now many different acceptable reasons for asking to adapt your working hours – for example, fitting in exercise, pursuing interests and hobbies, managing deliveries at home – compared with just a few years ago when many people felt they couldn't ask (and would have their requests turned down) if they weren't a working mother asking for childcare purposes.

#12 Foster time awareness at organizational, team and individual levels

In an ideal world, we'd all have complete control over our working time, and we'd be free from demands and interruptions – but that's not real life. By discussing our aspirations and frustrations openly, we can agree a better way of managing our time across the team or organization that works for everyone. Being 'time aware' means openly acknowledging our choices and constraints, experimenting and learning, and sharing the dilemmas we encounter in managing the multiple demands on our time. It's not rocket science, but it does require discipline and skill. By paying attention to all of these things *and* contracting explicitly with one another about how and when we're doing our work, we're building time awareness.

'Productivity isn't about where you work, it's about how you're managed.' The Chartered Management Institute hits the nail on the head here:[14] managers play a critical role in building time awareness. They can help team members focus on the priorities and invest their time more effectively by asking questions such as, 'What will help us to achieve what we need to deliver? What's getting in the way?' Managers can differentiate between false and true urgency. In *A Sense of Urgency*, John Kotter describes how we're caught up in a flurry of activity and time pressure to fulfil demands by our bosses or clients.[15] This false urgency drains energy through activity rather than channelling it into productivity. With true urgency, managers focus on the critical issues rather than commissioning busyness.

That takes care of the 'what', but we also need to consider the 'how'. When people are consistently working late to meet deadlines, or certain individuals are disempowered from contributing equally, it may be time to re-work your team processes. Managers can task the team with designing a better approach, encourage them to trial different possibilities, then help them hone it to perfection. For example, a senior leader realized her team was routinely sending her documents to review a few hours before a deadline. With further iterations and edits invariably required, this meant a late night for everyone. She called this out by saying: 'This is unsustainable. We have to change how we operate and move our boundaries or we'll never be efficient or productive.' So they planned more in advance, booked 'review time' in her diary and brought a printed copy to annotate together. After six months, these reviews took just 15 minutes.

Many businesses have embraced Agile working,[16] an organizational concept and set of practices with origins in software development. Among other things, Agile working promotes greater time and place flexibility and a sharper focus on outcomes. Large projects are broken down into smaller time-boxed increments of work called sprints; at the end of each sprint, the team conducts a 'retrospective' to review what worked well, what didn't and what could be improved in the next sprint. These Agile practices can help to build time awareness of how day-to-day work is delivered.

One minefield that managers have to navigate is the fact that team members will likely have different needs and preferences in terms of their working time. Parents may value time out early and late in the day; younger people may value time for networking and development; carers may need flexibility and back-up to cope with emergencies; others may wish to respect important religious or cultural traditions. Some of us are owls, others are larks; some like finishing a task well before a deadline, while others need a pressing deadline to get started. Here's how managers can resolve these differences in a harmonious and business-focused way.

#13 Create a time-savvy team

The crucial first step is to know what a sustainable, productive use of working time looks like for everyone, so encourage team members to share their preferences, either with you privately or, if there's a trustful environment, with one another. Sometimes there may be a particular trigger for doing this, such as one or more unfilled vacancies, a significant change in the team's workload or a change in someone's circumstances. For example, a senior legal and banking professional said:

During several months of ill-health, I was working half the time, but because my team knew *how* I organized my time, it led to better productivity and my being promoted. It took that experience for us to look at our days and say, 'Okay, we need to rethink the way that we work. We need to work smarter.'

Let's unpack 'working smarter as a team'. A team may complete different types of work activities every day, but ricocheting mindlessly from one activity to another is inefficient and depletes us cognitively; it is far more beneficial to group activities where possible. One morning a week might be set aside for strategic deliberations; one afternoon a month for reviewing work progress and individual performance. This can help prevent the important but less urgent activities being repeatedly postponed. In a survey, I asked people how much 'deep thinking' time they needed per week to do their jobs well.[17] On average, this was 15 hours a week, or 1.5 to two days. How much did they typically achieve? Two, three or maybe five hours a week at best. Deep thinking time kept being pushed to the bottom of the list.

Sometimes people shy away from raising the question of their working time because they think a change has to be big and formal. But often it's the small things that we can ask for and do for others that make a significant difference. By asking, 'What do you need to do your best work this week?' or 'How can I help you be more productive with your time?', we may be surprised at how often we can help.

#14 Develop a team time contract

How do you pull all of these conversations together into a cohesive whole? How do you ensure everyone has the same understanding of this, not multiple variations on a theme? One effective way is to develop a team time contract, where you invite colleagues to figure out the best way to collaborate across the team, keeping your business goals front of mind.

A team time contract sets out:

- what communication channels will be used for what purpose
- email response times
- 'no fly zones' for meeting-free time
- what warrants a meeting and what doesn't
- buddying and back-up arrangements
- what's delegated, by whom and to whom
- how time for learning and development is protected
- what informal social time is valued
- whether/how people may be contacted outside of working hours
- how downtime, exercise and deep thinking time will be signalled and respected.

In Appendix 4, you'll find a sample time contract to inspire your own discussions with your team.

Let's touch specifically on meetings – after all, we invest so much of our working time in meetings. These can be hugely productive, energizing interactions, and essential to people's learning and development. Equally, they can be the bane of our working lives and the number one drain on our productive working time. Here's why:[18]

'Attending endless meetings that have no purpose or output.'
'Meetings that go off-topic, are inefficient or unnecessary.'
'Large meetings where I'm only expected to listen.'
'Being expected to attend meetings that have nothing to do with my area.'

In-depth advice on running high-quality meetings abounds, so you won't find that replicated at length here. Instead, below are just five effective ways to make the best use of meeting time and a diversity of participants:

1. *Invest in systematic training for conducting efficient meetings.* Include this in development programmes and promotion criteria; consider accreditation for individuals.

2. *Be highly selective about organizing a meeting.* Is it for progress reporting, information-sharing, decision-making, problem-solving, creative thinking or team building? What are other ways in which you could achieve this purpose?

3. *Ensure everyone participates.* Relying on people speaking up favours majority groups and extroverts. Call on individuals by name, acknowledge everyone's input and call out repeat interrupters.

4. *Ask people to write down their position at the start of the meeting.* Invite people to share this in turn, *then* start the discussion, for a richer use of the diversity and knowledge represented.

5. *Initiate one word check-ins and check-outs.* At the start and end of the meeting, ask everyone to say just *one* word that describes how they are feeling. Don't discuss these or ask for elaboration. These help everyone to tune into the human/social dynamics as well as the task.

From the organization to the individual

We have looked at how to manage time more thoughtfully across teams and the organization as a whole. What about the individual? Well, we're all responsible for developing our own time awareness, speaking up and doing what we can to shape a healthier time culture wherever we work. This book is deliberately not focusing on individual time management, but if you're wanting some guidance on ways to manage time better in your own work life, there is a checklist to aid you in the toolkit in Appendix 4.

We do need to understand how to create a time culture that enables individuals to flourish at work and fulfil their potential. In the next chapter, we'll turn our attention to people and discover the time solutions for recruiting, managing and developing employees.

Chapter 8
Time and talent

Time solutions for recruiting, managing and developing people

This chapter explores:

- the changing 'time deal'
- *career committed* organizations
- *community cultivators*
- creating an integrated approach.

ORGANIZATIONS ARE RETHINKING how they manage and reward their workforces. Sourcing and growing skills, promoting wellbeing and strengthening social bonds have quickly risen to the top of the agenda as businesses strive to become more resilient and adapt more quickly to ever-changing circumstances. In this chapter, we'll delve into two more traits of time-focused organizations: being *career committed* and *community cultivators*. We will also discover the specific solutions that enhance people's work lives and careers, their wellbeing and their productivity. This is not about 'being nice' to employees; instead, it's about creating a win–win environment where individuals can give their best and the business can grow its bottom line.

The changing 'time deal'

What do employees today want from their employer in return for the hours they invest in their jobs? What do employers need to offer to attract and retain employees with desirable skills? Here are five ways in which the 'time deal' between employer and employee is changing.

1. *Longer-term careers.* While there will always be individuals who job-hop and businesses that slash headcount in a downturn, the pendulum is swinging slowly back towards greater job security. Organizations that are taking the 'S' of their ESG commitments seriously are maintaining continuity of employment by minimizing redundancies, and reskilling and redeploying people where possible.

2. *Personalization.* Employers are finally appreciating that their employees have different ambitions, needs and circumstances. To help every individual to give their best at work, they are seeking to personalize the 'employee experience' through more tailored working arrangements, career paths and benefits.

3. *Development.* Demand from both employers and employees for learning and development is rocketing. Some 94% of business leaders expect employees to pick up new skills on the job, up from 65% in 2018,[1] while registrations for online personal development courses grew a staggering 88% during 2020.

4. *Boundaries.* As the boundary between working hours and non-working hours has blurred, people want their full working time to be acknowledged and their time off to be protected. The time that the employee spends effectively 'at the employer's disposal' (often unpaid) is

coming under greater scrutiny, as businesses from Uber[2] to Goldman Sachs[3] have been discovering.

5. *Wellbeing.* Employers are now more involved in supporting people's wellbeing outside of the workplace. For example, the law firm Linklaters launched new support measures for any employees experiencing domestic abuse. Some 43% of employees want their employer to offer relationship support.[4] And when furloughed employees were unable to work during the pandemic, leading employers focused on supporting people's financial, emotional and physical wellbeing.

Overall, do people care more about time or money? The answer is interesting. On one hand, we typically undervalue time: only 48% of us would choose time over money.[5] However, 87% of employees want to work flexibly and one in four full-time workers would prefer to work part-time hours for less income *but only if this didn't affect their career progression.*[6] So when we do value time more than money, we're not prepared to accept limited advancement as the trade-off. How much we value time likely changes by life and/ or career stage too.

Career committed organizations

Against the backdrop of this evolving time deal, time-focused organizations are updating their approaches to job design, performance management and promotion, rewards, benefits, career management, and learning and development.

#15 Design time-flexible roles that cater for diverse preferences

Job design specifies what work needs to be done, other roles with which this role needs to work closely and *how* the work can be done. Different time-flexibility options include part-time, job-sharing, hybrid or term-time roles, and annualized or compressed hours. All bring advantages and challenges for both employer and employee, but it is possible to create time-flexible roles that meet the needs of different employees *and* the resourcing needs of the business.

We often forget to look across the whole year, yet reduced hours can be applied on an annual basis. For example if the job is designed to be 80% of a full-time role, then the 20% of non-working time could be banked and taken during school holidays or quieter business months. In consulting firms, people on 80% hours often take the 20% off between projects, for example. Another approach is to agree to focus on one aspect of the role for three to six months, then a different aspect for the next three to six months. This may work better for the individual while allowing the employer to respond to demand variation across the year. Roles tend to expand over time, business priorities change and the employee's situation may also change in terms of life stage, health, development or ability to travel. So *career committed* organizations refresh the job design regularly – at least annually – and collaboratively with the incumbent.

When advertising roles internally and externally, leading employers use the #happytotalkflexibleworking strapline[7] in *all* their advertising. They are also offering flexibility from day one (the legal right to *request* flexible working only kicks in at 26 weeks of employment) and granting requests for flexibility wherever possible, instead of looking for grounds for refusal. They use behavioural science to 'nudge' diversity when hiring,[8] by focusing on the goals rather than the years of experience required and by including prompts that encourage greater candidate diversity. For example, Zurich Insurance Group saw a 20% increase in female applications for management roles after advertising every role with flexible terms and gender-neutral language.[9] Some organizations have successfully created a role design and hiring toolkit for managers that lists all the possible time-flexibility configurations, example job designs and 'nudge' words to include in their job advertisements.

A common refrain among employees is that while jobs may be advertised as time-flexible, the employer's commitment to making this time-flexibility work well in practice is at best patchy and at worst, non-existent. One thing organizations can do to signal that they are serious about embracing time-flexible roles is to appoint a flexibility champion – ideally a partner or director with the clout to speak out, tackle barriers and advocate on behalf of others. People also need to see concrete evidence that it's possible for *someone like me* to progress up the career ladder in time-flexible roles, so *career committed* organizations make these examples visible across the organization.

#16 Stop looking at time as a measure of performance

Once you've prioritized your collective time investments as an organization, what then? How do you translate these priorities into meaningful goals for individuals and evaluate their performance? The answer – again – is to focus on outcomes *not* inputs: describe what will be delivered if the individual is working at optimum productivity, and assess their performance against that.

This may require you to shift away from using billable hours as your primary performance metric. If this sounds unfeasible, let's remind ourselves that fully remote work was deemed impossible pre-COVID. At the very least, performance metrics should take into account *all* that employees contribute to, not just client-chargeable work. Trial your new approach jointly with a supportive client who values innovation: pick a small contract, agree some target outcomes then evaluate performance against these afterwards. It *is* feasible and it's happening already – for example, one international law firm sets no billable hours targets for lawyers, focusing instead on the quality of client service. This strengthens their 'one firm' culture rather than a culture of individualism and internal competition.

Career committed organizations set a mix of short-, medium- and longer-term performance goals. Short-term goals help embed recent learning and build confidence in new skills; longer-term goals help an individual plan for their next promotion and demonstrate your commitment as an employer to their future career growth. In one professional services firm, every employee has a 'continuity' manager who attends all performance reviews with the line manager and employee, and takes a holistic view of the individual's progress and aspirations beyond their current role. *Career committed* organizations pay equal attention to the valuable non-financial contributions the individual has made, and 'how' they have delivered as well as 'what'. They include behavioural goals that exemplify the values and culture to which their organization aspires, and formally recognize time spent on diversity and inclusion activities and mentoring colleagues. This blending of 'what' and 'how' is mirrored in audit functions – for example, where auditors are increasingly looking to audit in different ways with much greater focus on staff and management behaviours.

Finally, *career committed* organizations are changing the way they gather and share performance feedback, by holding monthly performance discussions and encouraging on-the-job and just-in-time feedback. This has been proven to stimulate productivity and reduce procrastination. The annual review then becomes an opportunity to forward plan rather than go through a year's worth of feedback. One banking group has rebranded performance management as 'progression' management, and uses the annual review to identify specific ways to close skills gaps over the coming year. Leading organizations are also tackling time-bias in appraisals; time-bias is when people working in time-flexible roles receive consistently lower performance ratings compared to colleagues not working time-flexibly. By comparing appraisal outcomes across different groups of flexible workers as well as minority groups, we can spot unwanted patterns and take action where it's needed.

#17 Reward contributions in a timely, fair and personalized way

When incentivizing and rewarding employees, time-centric organizations are moving away from paying according to years of experience and competencies, and instead paying for work delivered and skills developed. They are focusing on more timely recognition of contributions and achievements, greater personalization and choice, and a strong regard for fairness, regardless of how different employees spend their working time. Here's how they are doing this.

First, they are paying for achievement – for the tasks completed, not the time spent on them. Some organizations are going as far as scrapping their annual pay review and instead awarding spot bonuses for specific tasks or projects. They are also rewarding collaboration, team-based working and inclusive behaviours with spot bonuses for high-performing groups; this is an effective way to reinforce a more collective approach to working time. As Noreena Hertz, broadcaster and academic, states in a *Financial Times* article, 'If we want the workplace to feel less lonely, part of the challenge is explicitly valuing qualities such as kindness, co-operation and collaboration... finding ways to reward and incentivize such behaviour.'[10]

Second, they are eliminating time bias in their rewards by calibrating pay decisions and tracking pay progression to ensure that time- and location-flexible employees are rewarded as fairly as those working full-time in offices. One example of how an organization is addressing time bias comes from a financial services organization that created a gender pay gap modelling tool for managers to use during the pay process so they could see the impact of different reward decisions immediately instead of waiting for the annual pay gap reporting cycle to roll around.

Third, they are adapting their pay philosophies to reflect the evolving patterns of work today and starting to pay according to where people spend their working time. As 'work from anywhere' is becoming mainstream, research by Willis Towers Watson finds that half of employers (49%) are designing a hybrid reward model and two in 10 (18%) are now setting pay levels by first determining the market value of an employee's skills and then applying a geographic differential based on where the employee is located.[11]

#18 Offer time-related benefits that employees value

The shift described above is impacting employee benefits too. Time-focused organizations are embracing 'flex wellbeing' and time-centric benefits that help every individual proactively maintain a healthy, sustainable work life.

Partly prompted by the many additional pressures placed on employees during the COVID-19 pandemic, employers are taking steps to help employees free up time to work productively by offering meeting-free days and weeks: Novartis mandated a meeting-free first week of the year to help people settle back into work productively and in spring 2020, Citigroup announced Zoom-free Fridays. As the length of the average working week rose 9% during 2020, firms began offering a corporate 'wellbeing' day off to thank employees for their hard work and to emphasize the importance of rest. For example, Unilever implemented a Global Day of Thanks in October 2020,[12] while Citigroup announced a company-wide holiday at the end of May 2021, acknowledging 'the need for a reset'.[13] Other organizations are letting employees choose when they take time off: insurance group Beazley added paid 'wellness' days off to existing annual leave entitlements, for example.

Short bursts of additional undisturbed time are being organized, such as 'firebreak' weekends where a Friday and Monday are mandated as meeting- and/or email-free to give people some quiet, productive time. In some cases, the two days are offered as additional paid leave. Longer stretches of paid leave are also being offered for a wider range of reasons than historically permitted, and being extended to all employees – not just parents – for myriad purposes, including travel, education or dealing with the unexpected. One consultancy offers three months' unpaid sabbatical to all employees regardless of length of service, while another consultancy's Time Out Programme offers one month's unpaid leave with no reason required. A global law firm offers 12 days' paid leave per annum for personal emergencies. Volvo, Aviva, the John Lewis Partnership and Diageo are among employers offering equalized paid parental leave to men and women to encourage greater sharing of caring responsibilities.

Flex wellbeing benefits include another emerging dimension relating to how employees spend their *non-working* time. For example, employers are helping people to minimize any emotional 'spillover' from their home lives into their work lives by facilitating access to relationship experts. Other companies are providing a personalized wellbeing budget. This is typically somewhere in the hundreds of pounds per person/per annum, and employees can spend their budget *on any activity outside of work* that promotes their wellbeing. This sends the signal that diversity of experience and time invested in outside interests are valued positively.

#19 Invest in lifelong learning, reskilling and building transferable skills

How do we apply the principles of collective time management to learning and development (L&D)? By making considered investments in people's ongoing acquisition of skills that are highly sought after by employers. There are individual benefits from greater employability and a more productive, longer-term career. There are business benefits from closing skills gaps, attracting a more diverse workforce and boosting income and profits. The proof? The top 5% of companies investing in people development increase their revenue *twice as fast* as the bottom 5% and their profits *1.4 times* as fast.[14]

When selecting leaders, *career committed* organizations are assessing the extent to which candidates have empowered their teams to adopt a healthy time culture *as well as* achieve their business results. Leadership development discussions typically focus on 'What are you achieving?', but a better question is, 'How can we help you manage your time better to achieve the important priorities?' Time-focused employers are also growing their future leaders early through leadership training workshops, time working on career plans and regular face-time with a coach/mentor. For example, PwC host a leadership retreat called 'Discover' for junior employees who have recently taken up their first managerial position. Here they learn about leadership skills, set career goals and identify progression opportunities.[15]

Time is also being factored into other development programmes, such as unconscious bias training, where the sheep-dip approach of herding all your employees through the same short, mandatory online courses is now recognized as having a very limited and even potentially a negative impact. Investing time in in-person training that explores difficult conversations is far more effective. Make sure your training includes unintended bias against different time-flexible work patterns, not just against protected characteristics.

This investment in lifelong learning and transferable skills helps people to move across job families and competency models, and enables the business to resource work in an agile way. L&D programmes are becoming more personalized, supported by data and technology *and* coaching time with managers. For example, 'passion' projects, where people can spend an agreed percentage of their working time on an initiative that is not directly related to their day job, can enhance people's sense of purpose, loyalty and creativity.

As an employee, keeping track of your completed training courses, certifications and development initiatives across your career can be cumbersome. The *Good Work* review points out that, 'As people move between jobs and through life it should be easier for them to talk about the skills they have developed along the way.'[16] One solution proposed by business leader and author Matt Nixon[17] is an enhanced online CV, which enables people to carry their training records, qualifications, feedback and psychometric evaluations from employer to employer. Why not take the lead and launch a talent or leadership passport in your industry?

#20 Support people's careers before, during and after their employment contract

Time-focused employers don't limit people's careers to the 'next step on the ladder' or 'while you are with us'; instead, they adopt a longer-term view over the full career life-cycle, acknowledging that people's ambitions vary by life stage, background and personal circumstance. They are committed to a multi-party investment of time, where the employer frees up more time for development; the manager coaches team members and HR provides the tools, data and technology platform. The individual owns and drives their own progression; one CHRO described this as 'being CEO of your career'.

Narrow recruitment criteria and recruiting from the same limited sources can act as a barrier to some groups.[18] By broadening the recruitment process and reaching young people earlier in their education, we can encourage a wider range of applicants. Feedback from solicitors of colour to the Law Society, for example, confirmed that talks from legal professionals at their school or college had a positive impact on their decision-making, particularly for those lacking role models.[19] Alongside school outreach initiatives, firms such as Nestlé, Barclays and JP Morgan are boosting the employability of young people through training and apprenticeships. They see this as a win–win situation, helping more school leavers/graduates into jobs and expanding the future talent pool for their industry.

Induction and onboarding programmes play a vital role in welcoming a new employee to the organization and helping them understand who's who and how things are done 'around here'. Traditionally, these programmes have focused on the factual element of roles, but advice on how to succeed in the company is greatly valued by new joiners. So clearly set out the different career paths available, the working time flexibility on offer and the positive time norms you encourage to help people to flourish in their careers.

While the salary and benefits you offer need to be competitive, professionals place a high value on time for physical networking. Some 72% of recent master's graduates believe the lack of physical networking would impact their longer-term progression, for example.[20] Face-to-face interactions, on-the-job development, 'working at the next level' projects and profile-raising opportunities all enable advancement for ambitious employees, but make sure these offers are made fairly and transparently. Time spent on formal sponsorship arrangements, secondments, coaching and various types of mentoring have proven effective in retaining and promoting employees, particularly in under-represented demographics. It's not just a 'nice to have' – clients are increasingly asking for evidence of this in selecting their service providers.

Clients are also getting inquisitive about your 'stay gaps'; this is the difference in length of service between groups of employees with different demographics in terms of ethnicity, gender, disability and so on. Analysing your stay gaps help you to identify which employees are failing to thrive in your organization and why, so you can address these cultural and career barriers.

Time-focused organizations are moving away from rigidly defined career paths and asking people what they want to have a shot at.

A part-time, location-flexible investment director speaks highly of her employer where, 'You say where you want your career to go, what your ambitions are, what you want to achieve over the next five years and they'll try and help you into those roles.' This manifests at the later stages of people's careers too, where employers are helping people in their fifties and sixties plan their final decade (or more) of work. They are jointly planning how the individual's role and time commitment might evolve – for example to become one element of a new portfolio career or to switch tracks from selling and managing work to taking on greater responsibility for developing others.

Community cultivators

Let's move on and look at the time solutions that help organizations to foster healthy, close-knit employee communities, encourage social bonds to flourish and create genuinely inclusive workplaces. Here I want to call out the glaring discrepancy between well-intended corporate wellbeing 'solutions' and the reality of many working environments. Remember those statistics on long working hours, burnout and stress from Part 1? The most effective way to promote good levels of physical and mental wellbeing among employees is *not to have a culture that depletes people so badly in the first place.*

During 2020, many employers rushed to roll out wellbeing initiatives to help employees cope with the pandemic. Now, 'it's about institutionalizing wellbeing – strategies not solutions,' observes Amanda Scott, head of the UK Talent and Rewards business at global people consultancy Willis Towers Watson. I believe wellbeing should not be seen as a set of benefits detached from people's daily experiences of work. So does Alex Soojung-Kim Pang, who says, 'The ultimate solution to a 70-hour week is not a mental health webinar or mindfulness programme.'[21]

#21 Base your wellbeing strategy on healthier collective time habits

The core of any wellbeing strategy should be the way we invest our working time thoughtfully and sustainably. Overwork, stress and burnout aren't just problems for individuals to overcome. Public Health England research confirms that, 'Changes to workload or working practices appear to reduce stressors and factors that can lead to burnout. There is some evidence to suggest that organizational interventions produce longer-lasting effects than individual approaches.'[22] Instead of leaving it to individual employees to fight burnout, let's address the organizational practices that are causing burnout in the first place.

Time-focused organizations are changing the rhythm of the working day and normalizing healthier working practices. At one firm, it's walking meetings; at another, it's an office-wide 15-minute 'silence' at 8.00 am every day for individual reflection. You can invite leaders and teams to try a few different approaches and find out what works best in your business. New topics are being broached too, such as effective brain functioning and how we can protect our cognitive health from overload. As a starting point, in your organizational research you can include a (self-reporting) question about the degree/frequency to which employees experience cognitive overload, so you can identify who is most at risk of neuro-depletion.

Another practical step is to offer time-awareness training to reinforce the positive time norms that maintain energy and productivity. Attendees can reflect on their personal values and priorities, pinpoint ways of working that help and hinder brain efficiency, and build self-awareness about their own time habits. There's a sample agenda for time-awareness sessions in the re-working time toolkit in Appendix 4. Open these sessions up to mental health champions to help them have conversations with people who are overloaded or struggling and, importantly, help escalate to leaders any organizational factors that are outside the individual's control.

Finally, a low-cost and effective way to support employees is to make available a simple, accessible toolkit to aid them in managing their working day as healthily as possible. This might consist of reminders to group together similar work activities, set fixed times for checking emails, allow transition time between calls and take frequent breaks, for example. It's not rocket science, but it's the act of making this visible every day that prompts people to stick to better habits.

Healthy time practices enable us to lift our heads up from our to-do lists and make conscious choices about what we invest our time in – even if this is for minutes not hours or days. We can choose to spend the first few minutes of a Monday meeting inviting people to talk about their weekends; to inquire how someone is doing when we notice they don't have their usual bounce; or to ask a quiet colleague for their view. Let's take a look at the time practices that enable us to notice each other, appreciate our differences and value our unique perspectives.

#22 Take time to ask, listen, notice and appreciate

Many organizations conduct annual workforce surveys and perhaps more frequent 'pulse' surveys to gauge employee sentiment. But to ensure individuals feel truly heard and valued on a day-to-day basis, we need to go further. An active listening strategy can help us systematically seek out people's contributions and experiences to complement our own limited world-views.[23] It's also a proactive way to include the voices of minority employees – and their allies' voices – in discussions and decision-making. One law firm's active listening strategy includes reverse mentoring for senior executives and one-on-one listening sessions, and every quarter, board members listen to an employee sharing their experiences of working at the firm.

Remember the 'emotional tax' experienced by minority employees described in Chapter 5? Nearly 60% of people of colour have experienced this,[24] while 35% of LGBTQ+ employees hide their sexual orientation at work for fear of discrimination.[25] Collectively, that's a huge investment of time spent on exhausting self-protection. Addressing this effectively requires a systemic approach to inclusion; we can start by acknowledging this tax exists, inviting conversations about it and listening respectfully to those who have experienced it. But to have an impact, we need to go beyond asking and listening and call out any exclusive or discriminatory talk or practices that we see or hear.

Valuing individuals also means understanding their ambitions and motivations, and helping them to find the purpose in their work; doing this successfully makes a difference to the company's bottom line. Some people will have a deep need to pioneer social change; others may find purpose in a stimulating job, enhancing skills, building work friendships or providing for loved ones. When our sense of purpose comes from our life outside of work, such as becoming a parent, employers can still acknowledge and support these goals. Taking the example of parenthood, employers are increasingly supporting employees' journeys to parenthood by partnering with organizations such as Fertifa[26] to provide cost-effective access to fertility experts, treatment funding and corporate education.

As well as formal policies and benefits, time to talk with other colleagues can be hugely beneficial for those looking to find their niche, connect with potential sponsors, achieve an important goal or overcome work or personal challenges. Employee networks provide valuable peer support as well as feedback to leaders on organizational issues and initiatives, and are usually run by volunteers. Time-focused organizations are recognizing the time commitment of employee network organizers in their job design and performance objectives. For example, at BAE Systems, network co-chairs formally spend 20% of their work time on their network commitments, and other steering group members spend around 10%. At Siemens, time spent on network activities is treated in the same way as core work.[27]

Brexit, Black Lives Matter and the COVID-19 pandemic have forced us to re-examine the value and meaning of our social connectedness. How do we overcome division and forge strong, inclusive communities? This isn't just a question for our national identities and the neighbourhoods in which we live, but also for our workplaces. What practices build social cohesion and community spirit in organizations? Examples include having spontaneous conversations that add richness to our day; hearing the human stories behind the professional facades; being able to read emotions and body language, not just emails and screens; and coming up with ideas that are better for having been brainstormed together. To build and maintain a strong culture, we need to make the most of physical co-working in the future by creating dedicated time and space for employees to connect; initiatives on which people can work together; shared updates; and organized social events.[28]

#23 Nurture that all-important human 'glue'

Storytelling is a powerful way to connect hearts and minds, so one strategy for building 'glue' is to create opportunities for people at all levels to share their personal stories. Internal communications are shifting away from structured, corporate 'push' towards more personal, employee-led 'pull' through real-time, personalized interactions. For example, at one organization the CEO posts twice-weekly videos to all employees. At another, the quarterly town hall gathering has become monthly, with the agenda set by a representative group of employees. A female business leader at a third organization told me how she stopped opening up her laptop during the day and 'carried it around like an accessory. I learnt that it didn't matter if I didn't look at an email or read a PowerPoint document.' She spends just 15 minutes a day on emails and the rest talking to people directly.

Another strategy for nurturing connectedness is pooling brainpower to bounce ideas around and jointly problem-solve; after all, 'a problem shared is a problem halved'. By crowdsourcing solutions, time-focused organizations are making it easier for colleagues to propose suggestions and develop innovative plans. At the law firm Linklaters, a partner set up a technology platform called The Ideas Pathway for colleagues worldwide to contribute ideas.[29] They run campaigns on specific questions, such as how to improve operating efficiency and how best to balance work and childcare, and 'Ideas Sprints' to collect great ideas that might otherwise be lost. This collaborative approach is critical if organizations are going to design solutions that genuinely work for their employees.

We can build 'glue' by encouraging people to express their identities, values and passions, and connect with like-minded colleagues. Setting up shared interest groups can achieve this goal; work-related topics might include tech sessions and mentoring book clubs for example, while the COVID-19 pandemic saw virtual messaging boards and meetings featuring cats, cooking, photography and more. Participating in group challenges or joint fundraising for a good cause also fosters pride in shared achievements, so tap into people's goodwill through volunteering initiatives. Organizations are discovering more informal ways to match internal expertise with colleagues looking for specific support, from reading with colleagues' children or running homework clubs to buddying up new parents with experienced ones.

Social cohesion flourishes when people genuinely feel they belong, in addition to feeling connected and sharing experiences with others. In a survey of 4,700 home-workers across six countries, flexible workers scored more highly on a sense of belonging to their organization than those on a nine-to-five schedule.[30] It's another compelling business reason to embrace flexible working for good: a better work–life balance means happier, more loyal employees who are willing to go the extra mile for their employer.

Creating an integrated approach

We've seen a multitude of ways now in which organizations can adapt and improve the way they manage time. Some of the solutions described above are quick and simple to implement, while others require careful planning, skilled resources and cross-functional support. In Chapter 9, we will see how two major businesses have successfully adopted differing approaches and draw some lessons from their experiences.

Chapter 9
Ahead of time

Organizations that are leading the way in managing time

This chapter explores:

- learning from the front-runners
- Case study 1: Building long-term business resilience
- Case study 2: Promoting work sustainability
- the common threads
- from answers to action.

Learning from the front-runners

THE PRECEDING CHAPTERS have set out the different ways in which organizations can make better use of working time, including the six traits in Chapter 6 and the time solutions detailed in Chapters 7 and 8. If you're still pondering how to put these ideas into action, then here's how two leading businesses, KBC Group and Zurich Insurance Group, are successfully re-working time in their organizations. They are 'fixing the system' by creating more productive, sustainable ways of working that allow people to focus on making a valuable contribution.

Case study 1: Building long-term business resilience

KBC Group[1] is a bank insurer headquartered in Belgium, with a workforce of 41,000 employees, who serve over 12 million customers across central Europe and South-East Asia. They help clients to save, invest and limit their risks, they provide loans and they fund industry projects. External drivers include low interest rates, global health risks, technological advancements and climate change, while the banking and insurance sectors are highly competitive with online banks, e-commerce operators and fintech companies all chasing a bigger slice of the pie.

KBC's strategy of 'Differently: The Next Level' focuses on long-term business resilience. They had already embarked on a major transformation to digitize their services and adapt to changing customers' needs before the pandemic struck; this simply accelerated their efforts. 'Differently' also means implementing what the company's Chief Human Resources Officer', Anette Bohm, calls 'a green policy for our employees'. Counter to banking sector norms of firing in a downturn then hiring afresh, they've explicitly committed to re-skilling and re-deploying their employees wherever possible. 'Our employees were very loyal to us in the crisis in 2008 and deserve to be treated fairly', reflects Anette.

They are committed to long-term outcomes

'Our investors are much more interested in the long-term development of the company than in the short-term and this helps us to focus on the longer term too.' Accordingly, KBC executives prioritize long-term client relationships and sustainable, profitable growth over short-term, high-risk/high-reward goals. One consequence of this longer-term mindset is that leaders take the time to seek out different perspectives and harness collective intelligence.

For example, the top 40 leaders regularly set aside time together to look at what is going on in the world. They hear from experts in different fields, discuss global trends and developments, and draw inspiration to influence their own business plans. The emphasis is firmly on collaboration, not competition. This is mirrored in their business values, which encourage collaboration and 'smart copying' across national borders.

They encourage 'freedom within a framework'

KBC values time spent helping people to understand their business strategy. Their CEO gives regular updates, which are followed up with a short survey asking employees how much they *understand* the strategy, how much they *support* it and how comfortable they are with its *impact* on them personally. Within this 'big picture' framework, local leaders help their teams to specify how they will contribute to these goals. 'We try to spend enough time with the teams to get clear commitments from them about what they will contribute during the year.' They have defined what productivity means for different functions and are increasingly turning to tech-enabled solutions to help free up people's time for higher value work. For example, the payroll team came up with the idea of adapting the customer chat bot to recognize and answer frequently asked payroll questions from employees. This approach requires a conscious balancing act: on the one hand, allowing people to experiment and take certain risks; on the other, encouraging people to stay productive and not lose sight of the 'here and now'.

They nurture social cohesion and psychological safety

If there is something that is really important in our company, it is social cohesion. We do many different things to bring people together and encourage friendships.

Being part of 'Team Blue' (the consistent colour across all the company's logos) is one way KBC unites employees across national boundaries. One 'Team Blue' challenge in May 2018 broke the Guinness World Record for organizing the world's largest online quiz with 1,129 employees participating simultaneously across six countries.

Why does KBC believe in the value of connecting people in their free time as well as on work-related activities? Because by creating strong social bonds, people feel more supported and are better able to cope under pressure. It benefits individuals and the business.

KBC has invested significant time in creating a psychologically safe environment: 'People need to feel safe in order to speak up with new ideas. We are fully aware that if we rely on innovation coming from the top down, this will take far too long.' KBC holds International Inspiration Days for employees on the same day in multiple countries. At these tech-enabled events, panellists from a diverse range of businesses discuss how they are staying ahead of industry developments and seed ideas among employees for improving the products and services they deliver.

During their transformation, KBC has aimed to 'take fear away' from the company's employees. If people's jobs disappear – for example, through branch closures – they are supported for 12 months to re-skill themselves, with access to job coaches who help them secure a new role.

They incentivize a better use of working time

Pre-pandemic, KBC employees already worked flexibly. Headquartered staff could work two days per week from home and individual working hours could be flexed between 6.00 am and 10.00 pm. Post-COVID, the company is embracing 50% homeworking across the business, with teams coming together physically two days a week. In adopting the principle of 'team first, then individual', KBC expects team members to contract with one another about new working patterns without compromising the service delivered to clients, and is boosting the skills of managers to lead these 'mature discussions'.

In its performance management process, KBC has moved away from traditional evaluations and towards 'progression dialogues'. The difference? These are more forward looking, with more time spent discussing what employees are/aren't *able* to deliver and how to enhance their skills. Less time is wasted on debating the validity of the performance evaluation itself.

KBC has also adjusted its rewards model by converting some variable pay into fixed pay and local allowances, and using the reduced variable element to recognize extraordinary contributions towards team goals. It publishes quarterly awards to help people understand what the important work is, what a valuable contribution looks like and what they can expect to receive in return for going the extra mile.

Case study 2: Promoting work sustainability

Zurich Insurance Group[2] is a global multi-line insurer that serves individuals, small businesses, mid-sized and large companies, and multinational corporations across more than 215 countries and territories. It reported business operating profits of US$4.2 billion in 2020.

> We care about our people. We want to sustain collaboration, team spirit and a positive working culture. We want to foster diversity and inclusion and we also want to contribute to societal sustainability.

This is how David Henderson, Group Chief Human Resources Officer, describes Zurich's work sustainability commitment. Zurich's corporate purpose is to 'create a brighter future together', emphasizing collaboration between employees, customers, consumers and communities. Here's why and how the company is managing time more strategically across its business.

It sees clear business benefits

By better matching the *nature* of work to *where* and *when* work gets done, Zurich is able to increase productivity. By offering greater time flexibility, the company is able to draw on a more diverse talent pool, which 'opens up more opportunities for us'. And from a wellbeing perspective, it can help to reduce fatigue, improve collaboration and connect people more effectively.

It is transforming its core processes

Zurich is simplifying and digitizing its business operations. For example, it is standardizing its products for small and medium-sized business customers; its Customer Intelligence Platform consolidates customer data into one place; and it has reduced the time it takes to conduct live claims assessments from 10–15 days to just 15–30 minutes.

It is reshaping working patterns

Zurich learnt during the pandemic that while the switch to remote working happened smoothly, many employees still needed to meet in person to feel their best at work. As pandemic-related restrictions continued to ease, they started to come back together physically in the group, closely aligning with local regulations. Zurich continues to look into a hybrid work model to explore different types of work and when/where these can be done, along with clear roles and responsibilities: 'Managers and employees have to be very thoughtful about this, so that they can determine how they use their working time to best advantage.'

Layered on top of this hybrid-working model is the time flexibility on offer. As part of Zurich's global FlexWork@Zurich programme, all roles are advertised as available part-time, full-time or on a job-share basis. At Zurich, 70% of employees make use of a flexible working arrangement and a remarkable 94% are happy with their work–life balance.

It is investing in longer-term careers and cross-business resourcing

Zurich has adopted a 'build' strategy for the skills and resources needed for the future and is growing these in house as much as possible, offering greater job security to employees in the process.

For example, the company set out to future-proof 3,000 UK workers – two-thirds of Zurich's UK workforce – with a £1 million upskilling programme to retrain them for future roles in areas such as robotics, data science and cybersecurity over a five-year period. Zurich's learning and development programmes help people move across job families, supported by 'MyDevelopment', a global digital learning platform. Employees are encouraged to become the 'CEO of your career'.

From a resourcing perspective, Zurich's Talent Marketplace platform enables managers to submit 'talent requests' for critical work where additional skills are needed. These requests are then matched with an employee who has the relevant skillset.

Performance management, pay and benefits

Zurich's approach to performance management, pay and benefits is changing too. The company is moving away from forced rankings and differentiated rewards, and towards more team-based rewards that incentivize collaboration. The company's time-off policies are generous and designed to support individuals in a variety of circumstances.

For example, Zurich offers equalized, enhanced maternity, paternity and adoption leave, with up to 16 weeks on full-pay for all parents, regardless of gender. Additional paid leave entitlements support employees undergoing IVF, giving birth prematurely, experiencing miscarriage and experiencing other bereavements.

For a business of this size in today's uncertain environment, living up to the ambition of 'being a caring employer' is no mean feat. How has Zurich brought all of this to life?

A thoughtful, evolving approach to implementation

The company is building on the progress it has made over recent years in fostering a culture of flexibility and trust, and starting to digitize its operating model. It has moved away from top-down, leader-led change and prescriptive policies. Zurich recognizes that a 'one-size-fits-all' approach won't work, not least because different countries and business units are at different starting points. Instead, it sets out clear principles that define 'the Zurich way' and encourages local business units to customize this to fit their markets and customers.

For example, it is establishing group-wide principles for its new hybrid-working model. These require teams to be physically co-located one or two days per week: 'The manager has a role to play in stipulating that, talking to team members and together working out how they will organize it.' They are embedding the principles with the 'three Ts: tools, training, technology'. The technology helps managers to plan for the time they need to be in the office and the workspace they require. The training builds managers' skills in managing hybrid-working teams while a variety of tools gives the whole team practical support to adapt to these new ways of working.

Their positive progress is evident across a range of organizational measures from their Organizational Health Index and employee Net Promoter Scores, where gaps in gender responses have closed, to enhanced levels of engagement across diverse groups of employees.

For David, the success of their continued transformation boils down to two things. The first is high levels of trust: 'in the last 12 months, more than ever, we've learned we can really trust our people to do the right thing, to step up and be counted on. We trust our people to be there for our customers and to be there for each other when needed.' The second is an open mindset: 'It takes a lot of careful planning and foresight and we're still learning.'

The common threads

While KBC and Zurich are rightly pursuing their own business strategies, serving their different clients in different ways, some common learnings emerge from the case studies:

- Establish a firm foundation with your business principles and values.
- Define 'the important work to be done', then ask 'What's the best way to deliver this?'
- Find new ways to serve clients that create operational and workforce flexibility.
- Don't insist on people being in the office every day, from dawn till dusk. 'We'll lose clients if we don't' is an excuse based on short-termism.
- Re-work time based on team first, individuals second.
- Encourage experimentation, risk-taking and innovation – within boundaries. People still need to deliver the important day-to-day work.
- Generate fresh thinking and enrich wellbeing by making time for creativity, external stimulation and connection.
- Promote collaboration, not competition, with team-based rewards.

These themes resonate strongly with Joris Wonders, managing director of Willis Towers Watson's Talent and Rewards consulting business in Western Europe, which advises major UK, international and global businesses across a range of industries.

He sees the shift from focusing on inputs to outputs accelerating, with companies increasingly looking at what people are achieving rather than where and when the work effort happens:

> In parallel, we're seeing a liberalization of attitudes with regard to time flexibility in working patterns. Previously, people often had to put forward a case when requesting a flexible arrangement and more often than not, this was based on child-care responsibilities. Now, the reason doesn't matter. It can be to pursue outside interests or simply for lifestyle reasons – these are seen as equally valid.

However, re-working time in a global organization brings certain challenges and complications. With cultural norms and legislative frameworks varying significantly by region, it's difficult for companies to adopt a single standard globally. 'These variations can cause genuine issues at the team level when you have people working together virtually who are based in different countries,' comments Joris. To overcome this, companies need to be clear about their intent – the same *direction* of travel for everyone – while recognizing that locations will progress at different speeds.

Time-focused organizations are also recognizing that quality work can't be sustained at top speed all the time. Slower-paced work is needed between bursts for teams to pause, digest and reflect; the same is true at the individual level. 'When we're switching rapidly between calls and different work activities, we're also switching between modes of behaviour,' reflects Joris. 'If you're making that switch once the next activity has started, you've already got it wrong.' For leaders, this could mean you're still in directing mode when enquiry mode is needed, or advisers may be bypassing listening and diving straight into problem-solving. Organizations that are addressing this effectively are encouraging people to manage their work day so they have time to assimilate, prepare and consciously shift into the right mode for the next activity.

From answers to action

In Part 2, we've discovered the six organizational traits of organizations that value and manage time strategically. We've also seen how leading companies bring these six time traits to life through specific practices and policies. Through these two case studies and many other examples, we've explored how a systemic, rather than piecemeal, approach is needed to address our broken culture of working time. Only by reassessing every aspect of the organization – structure, leadership, processes, resourcing, technology, people management and community – can we identify the right levers to pull on in order to successfully change the way we operate. Many companies talk positively about their excellent commitments and initiatives; of course, what matters most is *how successfully those intentions are translated into reality*, into day-to-day behaviours and people's experiences at work.

By now, you might be feeling clearer about the kinds of actions you could take to re-work time and genuinely shift the culture in your own organization. If you're wondering where to start, what order to tackle things in and how to build support for your plans, Part 3 addresses all of this. It explains how to diagnose your own time defects, get re-working time on the business agenda, prioritize and sequence your plan of action, and sustain momentum over the longer term, with tools and examples that you can borrow with pride. Let's get planning.

One-minute summary of Part 2

1. The six traits of time-focused organizations are: *outcome obsessed; deliberately designed; actively aware; career committed; community cultivators;* and *expertly evolving.*
2. These characteristics drive improved retention, creativity, diversity, belonging, wellbeing and ownership, and contribute to greater business resilience, productivity, agility and innovation.
3. Businesses can:
   - adopt a more strategic mindset and approach to managing time
   - simplify the organizational set-up to free up working time
   - create healthier time cultures by designing productive environments, giving employees more autonomy and building time-awareness.
4. The time deal between employer and employee is changing.
5. Organizations are supporting people's careers over the longer term, fostering healthy, close-knit employee communities and encouraging social bonds to flourish.
6. KBC Group and Zurich Insurance Group are two businesses that are successfully re-working time by creating more productive, sustainable ways of working that allow people to focus on making a valuable contribution.

Part 3
Time to act

How to re-work time in
your organization

Chapter 10
Taking stock of time

How to diagnose your time defects and get re-working time on the agenda

This chapter explores:

- time data and how to gather it
- evaluating your time data
- how to get this on the agenda in your business
- building the case for change
- from commitment to a clear plan.

S O WHERE TO start? The first step is to understand what your current approach to time management is, assess how well it is working for your business and get leaders talking about how you might re-work time in your organization. This chapter will help you to identify and gather the information, data and examples you need to put together a business case for change. Some of this may exist already in one form or another; you may need to supplement it with some additional targeted research. The data will help you to answer questions such as:

- How well do you currently value and manage collective working time?
- To what extent is your organization suffering from time blindness?
- What are the issues that are causing time defects in your organization?
- What are the building blocks you can use as a foundation for further improvements?
- How do we get this on the business agenda?

How you use this chapter and Chapter 11 may vary depending on your role, expertise and what guidance you're looking for. If you're an experienced organization development (OD) professional or change leader, you may want to selectively choose tools from this chapter to complement other models and approaches you've used in the past. If creating organizational change is newer territory for you, you may prefer to work through all the tools in turn; these two chapters offer you a practical handbook to guide your planning and action over the coming weeks and months.

Time data and how to gather it

To gain a true picture of how well you collectively manage and value time, it's important to gather a rounded, robust set of data. You will need to listen to other voices and perspectives that may be different to your own views and experiences. You'll benefit not just from hearing about what's broken and needs fixing, but also from crowd-sourcing ideas for potential improvements. Both quantitative and qualitative data play their part; you'll need to back up your findings with facts and figures *and* draw on individual stories and quotes to add depth and impact to your case for change.

Do you initiate an organization-wide data-gathering exercise? Or do you start small and then widen the lens over time? It depends partly on how receptive you believe the business will be to the idea of re-working time, and partly on what other strategic or organizational initiatives are planned over the coming months that this effort might support. If you've got some support already at senior levels, then go large! If you suspect a particular area of the business is either feeling the impact of a broken time culture, or conversely benefiting from a local approach that is working well, then use this as your starting point.

Let's look at four ways to gather data: survey questions, focus groups, a time blindness diagnostic and other organizational metrics. The first two assess the employee experience; the second two look more at how things get done and your 'current state'.

Surveys

With surveys, if you already conduct regular employee or organizational research, then you can add in some of the questions below. If not, you could design a short 'pulse' survey specifically for this purpose. You'll need to communicate clearly why you are gathering this data, how the responses will be shared with people and what action they might expect to see taken as a result. Potential questions to ask people include:

1. To what extent do you feel you have adequate autonomy over your working time in order to fulfil your role effectively?
2. To what extent do you feel you have adequate control over your working time to help you maintain your energy and wellbeing?
3. How do you feel about time at work? Please give one word or a short phrase to describe this.
4. On average, how much mental energy do you have during the working day? Please rate this between 1 and 10 where 1 is minimum energy and 10 is optimum energy.
5. What percentage of your working time is spent in meetings, on average?
   a. Of this, what percentage is spent productively?

    b.   And what percentage is spent unproductively?

6.   Please rate the extent to which you agree or disagree with the following statements (*Strongly disagree/disagree/neither disagree nor agree/agree/strongly agree*).

    a.   Busyness is celebrated and prized here.

    b.   I am able to set clear boundaries between my working time and non-working time.

    c.   During my non-working time, I'm doing a low level of work all the time.

    d.   I feel I have to invest additional time in my work in order to access the same opportunities as other colleagues.

Focus groups

Focus groups bring small numbers of employees (typically 10–20) together for a facilitated, open discussion. If survey questions tell you the 'what', focus groups explain the 'why'. The aim is not to respond to people's comments or provide answers, but to listen carefully, probe for examples and record their views. Make sure your focus group participants are representative of the wider workforce and to encourage openness; it is best to avoid having direct reports in the same discussions as their managers. Figure 10.1 provides a sample discussion guide that you can use or adapt.

Figure 10.1 Focus group guide

1. **Introduction**
   - The purpose of this session and how it will run
   - Confidentiality and ground rules
   - How the focus group data will be used
   - When participants will hear further

2. **What's the deal around working time here?**
   - What are you expected to give?
   - What do you expect to receive in return?

- Is this deal explicit or implicit? Why?

3. **How would you describe our time culture here?**
   - What words would you use?
   - What examples can you share?

4. **Reflecting on how we typically spend our working time:**
   - What helps you work productively? (positive time practices)
   - What gets in the way? (time defects)

5. **Which positive time practices could be replicated more widely across the organization?**

6. **How would you rank these time defects in terms of their impact on your productivity, career progression and wellbeing?**

7. **What improvements could help us all make better use of our working time?**
   - Prompts: work processes; decision-making; collaboration; people management and development; working patterns; data, tools and technology

8. **Close**
   - Is there anything else you'd like to mention or ask that is relevant to this session?
   - Thank people for their contributions

Time blindness

If you're wondering how much your organization suffers from time blindness, you can use this next diagnostic tool, the time blindness diagnostic (Figure 10.2), to find out. It's a light-touch way to get the conversation going and help you identify where to focus your efforts.

Figure 10.2 Time blindness diagnostic

How often do you...?

1. Talk about longer-term goals for the business, teams and individuals?
2. Talk to people about what's important, not just urgent?
3. Ask employees what helps/hinders them in focusing on the important work?
4. Discuss as leaders how you spend your time?
5. Articulate what a productive day looks like?
6. Simplify your organizational structure?
7. Review core work processes to reduce complexity and variations?
8. Look at end-to-end processes across business units?
9. Road-test ideas and proposals with different stakeholders?
10. Track how long it takes to make and communicate decisions?
11. Review job specifications and resourcing models?
12. Assess whether your tools and technology are helping people work and collaborate more efficiently?
13. Talk about the benefits of downtime and informal time at work?
14. Share stories about positive ways of managing time at work?
15. Experiment with new ideas instead of sticking with the status quo?

1 = Rarely or never; 2 = Occasionally; 3 = Regularly.

Total score:

15-25: You're in serious danger of ignoring your time culture completely. It's likely your organization is suffering from norms and defects that are hampering progress towards your business and people goals. It's time to start paying attention to these issues.

26-35: You're probably aware of some of the issues that are preventing you from making the most of your collective working time, but haven't fully grasped the nettle. What's holding you back from tackling known defects or upping the pace of change? Nail your business case and use early wins to gain some momentum.

36-45: You're highly tuned in to collective working time and you minimize organizational distractions so people can work productively and with energy. You're nimble and adapt to social and business drivers. You're ahead of the field in fostering a positive time culture.

Other organizational metrics

Finally with other organizational metrics, there are three important areas to mine for data: wellbeing, careers and time flexibility. In terms of wellbeing data, you can draw relevant questions from established measurement tools such as the Perceived Stress Scale, the Utrecht Work Engagement Scale and the Oldenburgh Burnout Inventory.[1] These assess cognitive functioning, physical and mental states and time spent experiencing positive emotions at work. As a guide, look for questions that explore how well people feel they manage the various demands on their time, how often they feel overwhelmed by these demands and how much energy (physical and/or mental) they have at work and outside of work. Protracted overwork and time pressure often drain people's resilience, so look for questions that ask people how emotionally resilient they feel at work and explore how well they are switching off from work.

With regard to careers, you can review your recruitment, career and exit data to glean some insights about your time culture. You should be able to spot some patterns and anomalies by analysing the following:

1. How does the wording of your job advertisements impact the diversity and quality of your applicant pool?
2. How long do people stay in your organization? Compare by age, race, gender, sexual orientation and other diversity factors.
3. Where do people tend to get stuck career-wise and why?
4. What aspects of your time culture are causing people to drop out or move on?

In your data-gathering effort you will need to include some hard facts around the time flexibility you offer as an organization, who benefits and who doesn't. Who is able to work in a time-flexible way? Look at different diversity cuts such as gender, race, sexual orientation, caring responsibilities, age and seniority. How does the percentage of people working in a time-flexible way compare across teams, departments, levels and business units? You can also compare the career and pay progression of those in time-flexible roles versus those who work in time-fixed roles.

Evaluating your time data

The next step is to evaluate all of this data and start to shape it into a coherent narrative. You are aiming to clearly articulate your current time culture, diagnose its strengths and weaknesses, explain who it is impacting most and how, and highlight the organizational opportunities and issues where you will need to target your efforts. These next three tools – the time management map, the time culture audit and the time impact assessment – will help you to accomplish all of this.

You will draw all your findings into a formal business case for change in due course; we'll cover this later in this chapter. But as you crunch the numbers and absorb the feedback, you'll be starting to get collective time management into your organizational language, and this is important. You're building understanding, bit by bit, about potential ways to re-work time to help people deliver their best work and maximize business performance.

Time management map

Let's look first at the time management map (Figure 10.3). This tool enables you to assess how your organization currently stacks up against the six traits of time-focused organizations that we examined in Chapter 6. You can take a first pass at this on your own, discuss it on a one-to-one basis with a few colleagues or work through it more formally in a workshop or dedicated session with a diverse group of colleagues to bring in multiple perspectives. First, identify where your organization sits presently on each continuum based on the data you have gathered. Then determine where your organization needs to be in future. The value of this tool lies in the conversations it will generate: it will guide your discussion about the ways of working and organizational design that you need to reach your business goals. We'll come back to this, and other tools, later on as you secure senior leaders' support and plan your implementation strategy.

Figure 10.3 Time management map

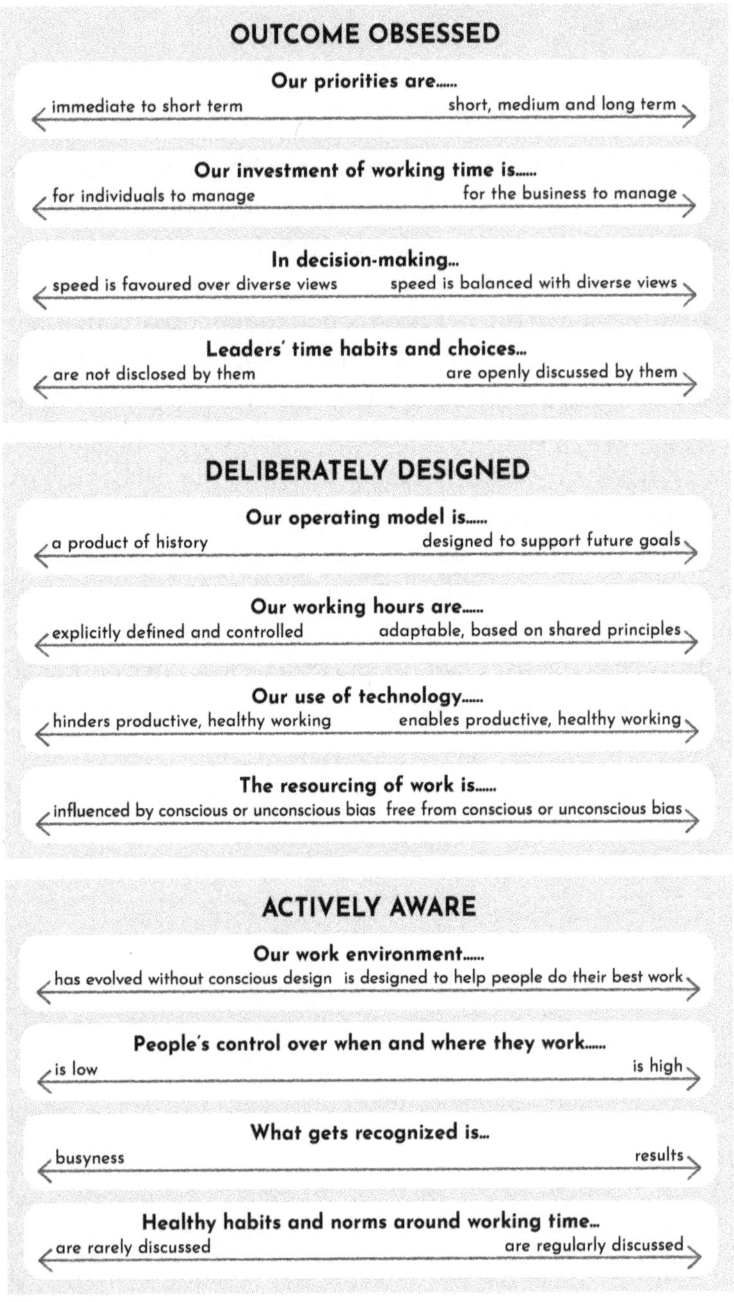

OUTCOME OBSESSED

Our priorities are......

immediate to short term ← → short, medium and long term

Our investment of working time is......

for individuals to manage ← → for the business to manage

In decision-making...

speed is favoured over diverse views ← → speed is balanced with diverse views

Leaders' time habits and choices...

are not disclosed by them ← → are openly discussed by them

DELIBERATELY DESIGNED

Our operating model is......

a product of history ← → designed to support future goals

Our working hours are......

explicitly defined and controlled ← → adaptable, based on shared principles

Our use of technology......

hinders productive, healthy working ← → enables productive, healthy working

The resourcing of work is......

influenced by conscious or unconscious bias ← → free from conscious or unconscious bias

ACTIVELY AWARE

Our work environment......

has evolved without conscious design ← → is designed to help people do their best work

People's control over when and where they work......

is low ← → is high

What gets recognized is...

busyness ← → results

Healthy habits and norms around working time...

are rarely discussed ← → are regularly discussed

CAREER COMMITTED

Our time deal is......

← opaque   transparent →

We support people's careers......

← during their time here   before, during and after their time here →

Our mindset towards external stakeholders is......

← transaction-based   eco-system-based →

Our people management processes are...

← time-based   outcome-based →

COMMUNITY CULTIVATORS

Managers are predominantly selected for their......

← technical skills   people management skills →

We value most the time that we spend......

← completing work tasks   fostering social connectedness →

The impact of working practices on people's wellbeing is......

← rarely reviewed   actively managed →

We recognize...

← some contributions more than others   all contributions equally →

EXPERTLY EVOLVING

In terms of the ways we work......

← we are cautious about change   we strive to continuously improve →

We favour...

← tried-and-tested approaches   experimentation and learning →

In discussions we value......

← consensus   dissenting voices →

Managers generally...

← control work tasks   delegate to team members →

How do you bring all the data, stories, examples, anecdotes and evidence together in a way that is concise and easily digested? You need a simple, effective way of summarizing this so people can quickly understand your time culture and share it with others.

Time culture audit

The next tool, the time culture audit (Figure 10.4), helps you describe your current time norms, what's driving these and how helpful or otherwise they are from a business perspective.

Figure 10.4 Time culture audit

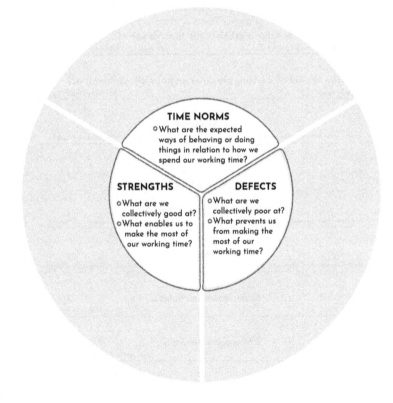

ORGANIZATIONAL EXAMPLES

What is the evidence?

TIME NORMS
- What are the expected ways of behaving or doing things in relation to how we spend our working time?

STRENGTHS
- What are we collectively good at?
- What enables us to make the most of our working time?

DEFECTS
- What are we collectively poor at?
- What prevents us from making the most of our working time?

In the top inner segment, list your time norms: your implicit or explicit ways of working that describe 'the way things are done around here' – for example, 'It is harder to progress in your career here if you have taken periods of extended leave.' Refer back to Chapter 2 for some common time norms. What is your data telling you about yours? In the strengths inner segment, list the positive practices and capabilities evident in your data, those things that your organization collectively does well – for example, 'We have a high retention rate due in part to our generous and flexible time-off policies.' In the defects inner segment, identify the areas of weakness that prevent people from working productively and healthily – for example, 'Employees of colour have fewer opportunities than their white peers to network with potential sponsors and mentors who could help them progress their careers.' Finally, in the outer segments, add in specific examples of how your organizational set-up *causes or reinforces* these time norms, strengths and defects – for example, 'Career paths are based on time spent at each level', or 'Managers feel uncertain about offering promotions to newly returned working parents.' As you work through the tool, you may find the following prompts useful: leadership; governance; decision-making; structure; processes; tools and technology; people management; environment; rewards; behaviours; values.

Time impact assessment

Understanding the impact of your time culture on different groups of employees is essential if you want to foster a more inclusive way of managing time at work that enables everyone – whatever their gender, age, background or socioeconomic status – to contribute, be heard and deliver their best work. The following time impact assessment tool helps you evaluate who's benefiting from your current approach to managing time, who's disadvantaged and how. It also tells you where to target your efforts over the coming months and how much cross-business coordination will be needed.

First, use Figure 10.5 to describe how groups of employees are impacted differently. You might identify different groups according to gender, age, race and ethnicity, social background, health and disability, sexual orientation, working pattern, caring responsibilities, seniority of role, length of service, client-facing/ support function or business-critical future skills. Don't forget to consider the intersections too – for example, minority ethnic graduates, mid-career employees living alone, senior female managers in client-facing roles. Drawing on the data you have gathered, summarize the impact of your current approach to managing time on each demographic group. How is it affecting their ability to work productively and progress in their careers? What changes are they saying would be beneficial? Are these changes within their own control or their team's control, or does ownership rest elsewhere in the organization? Once you've completed this initial analysis, plot your different employee groups on the four-box grid according to whether (1) the impact on them is positive, neutral or negative; and (2) potential improvements can be implemented locally or require a coordinated, organization-wide approach.

The results tell you where to focus your efforts. In the *top right* box, swift action could yield meaningful results in a short space of time. In the *bottom right* box are priorities to flag up to senior leaders that will likely require a more joined-up approach. In the *top left* box, find out what's important to keep here and whether any of these positives can be replicated for other groups or in other areas. And in the *bottom left* box are your organizational strengths – how can you bring groups in the bottom right box across to here?

Figure 10.5 Time impact assessment tool

Group description	Impact of current way of managing time	Potential improvements	Local, divisional or organization-wide
Entry-level graduates	o Negative o Excessively long working hours, little control over work o Difficult to progress quickly o Low retention rate beyond 2 years	o Flexible leave between projects o Job shadowing and early leadership skills programmes o Sponsors from different business areas	Divisional

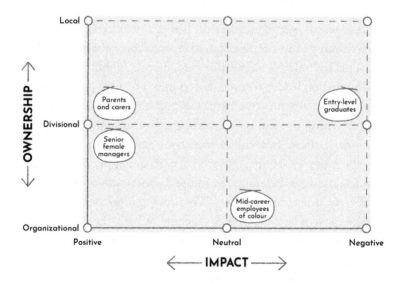

How to get this on the agenda in your business

Gathering good-quality data, analysing it and identifying the priorities is essential groundwork. But to make change happen, we have to secure leaders' active support. Let's pause to remember why this is so important. First, and most obviously, some of the changes that are needed may be organization-wide and quite strategic in nature. This is ultimately about achieving your business goals, so you'll likely need consensus at the most senior levels to taking action. Second, research has proven that leaders have a critical influence on people's behaviour. In *Organizational Culture and Leadership*,[2] Edgar Schein identified the top six drivers of positive change as:

1. what leaders pay attention to, control and measure
2. how leaders react to critical incidents
3. how leaders distribute resources
4. leader role modelling and coaching
5. how leaders reward people
6. how leaders manage people in, up and out.

In other words, getting leaders on board and actively committed to re-working time is essential to persuading others to follow suit. This isn't always straightforward, as one highly experienced transformation leader commented to me: 'The OD [organization development] work is not hard. Getting leaders over the line is hard.' Figuring out the issues, pulling a plan together, designing solutions… these 'rational' elements are much easier to achieve than the more 'emotional' aspects of persuading people that they need to do things differently in future. Leaders will want to know answers to questions such as, 'Why does this matter? Why is it urgent? How will the business benefit? What's the cost of not taking action? What are the risks involved?' And most importantly, 'What does it mean for me personally?' So the next step is to set out all of this clearly in a business case for action.

Building the case for change

How do you get re-working time on the table for discussion? Well, there may be more than one way into a formal conversation with leaders. Perhaps you've had a recent conversation with one senior leader that has touched on issues you've already identified. Or leaders may be focusing on a knotty business or organizational goal that would clearly benefit from a better use of working time. The 'hook' will vary depending on your business, your strategy, your current performance and your workforce. When setting out your case for change, three key points to bear in mind are:

1. *Make this about the business.* What are you collectively trying to achieve? Re-working time may feel like a difficult or intangible concept for people to get their head around, so be specific about how re-working time is going to help the business succeed.

2. *Frame this as an urgent problem.* We've already seen how we're hard-wired to prefer the status quo because we fear what change will cost us. To get people on board, we need to create dissatisfaction with the present, a compelling vision for the future and some clear first steps. You may be familiar with the 'Beckhard Equation' developed by David Gleicher and popularized by Richard Beckhard,[3] which describes a simple and memorable equation for this.

3. *Nail your messaging.* What are the most important points you want leaders to take away from this discussion? These should cover the 'what' and the 'how':
   - *What:* This is about achieving critical business goals, creating an inclusive workplace, finding more productive ways of working and building commitment, energy and resourcefulness among our employees. Appendix 2's 'Thirty arguments' can help you here.
   - *How:* This is not a one-off, box-ticking exercise; it's about how we deliver the important work in our business. It's an ongoing strategy and will require

persistence. It will also require leaders to communicate and role model the changes that are needed.

What really helps people to grasp what you're saying is framing the key points in a concise, visual way. You may need to draw on the underlying data for evidence to convince any doubters, but the true value lies in having a high-quality discussion, not in perfecting a long, written document.

Business case template

The business case template in Figure 10.6 helps you to set out your business case for change clearly and succinctly. In order to get people's commitment to change, we need to speak to their heads *and* hearts by blending the rational with the emotional, and the organizational with the personal. We have to draw on robust business data *and* impactful stories, and answer the questions 'What does this mean for the *business*?' and – critically – 'What does this mean for *me*?'

To use this tool, start with your business strategy and goals, and summarize those in the top box. The rest of the business case will set out how re-working time will help you achieve these. Summarize the data you have gathered into a few concise points. What is your current approach to managing time at work? What's working well and what's broken? Next, the 'So what?' Why does this matter? What's the negative impact on your business and your workforce? What are your organizational strengths and the opportunities on which you can capitalize? Then describe the change that is needed in terms of the *outcomes* you want to see: you're painting a compelling vision for the future here. Name the benefits and how you will measure these. Any business leader will also want to know what the risks are and what it's going to cost to implement this change. Finally, what are the first steps to take? You don't need to argue the 'how' here, the main goal of the business case is to frame the 'what' and to agree the need for change.

Figure 10.6 Business case template

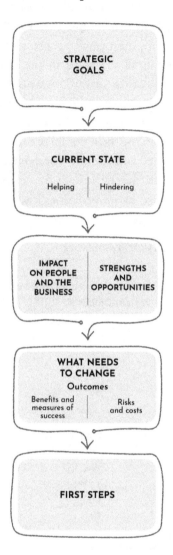

Traffic light framework

Remember that to successfully change the way things are done, we need to look at the situation holistically. When we understand how the different aspects of the organization are influencing or reinforcing the way we manage time, we can adjust those aspects that are leading us towards unhelpful outcomes and replicate other aspects that are yielding positive results. Imagine the organization as a fleet of ships. If some ships are pointing in the wrong direction, the overall progress of the fleet will be hampered. By aligning all the ships in the same direction, the whole fleet can move swiftly forward towards its destination. The traffic light framework shown in Figure 10.7 helps you to assess what's aligned and what's not; it helps you gain a clear view of what's going on in even the most complex organization. This tool and the business case template are complementary. Unlike the business case template, the traffic light framework doesn't set out the vision for the future; however, it does lead you further into the 'how' of re-working time.

Figure 10.7 Traffic light framework

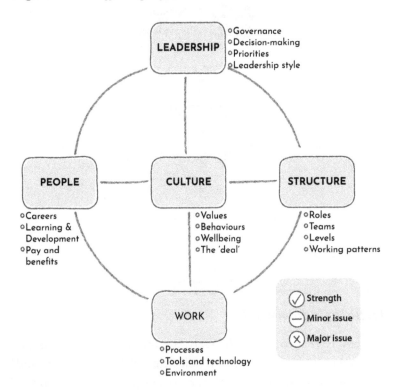

Start with the box on 'Leadership'. What do your data say about the way the organization is led? Include any findings about governance, decision-making and leadership behaviours next to this box. Then move onto 'Structure'; here, add in any data relating to how people and the work are organized. And so on. Next, add the traffic lights: green, or a tick, for positives to build on or replicate; amber, or a dash, for minor issues that are not widespread; red, or a cross, for major issues that are affecting the whole organization and/or significantly impeding business performance. Once completed, the framework will show you at a glance where to focus your collective efforts, both in resolving defects and spreading successes.

From commitment to a clear plan

If you have worked through your data, prepared and shared your business case and secured leaders' commitment to finding a better way to manage working time across the organization, congratulations! That's great progress. The next big question is, 'What should the plan of action look like from here?' You'll already have a sense of what you need to focus on in your organization. The next chapter digs down into the detail: how exactly you can design and implement a better way of managing time. It explains how to engage other people as you're building your plan so that this becomes a collective effort. You'll also discover what successful strategies for re-working time look like and how to position your own strategy alongside other organizational priorities and initiatives.

Chapter 11
Time strategies

How to implement time solutions successfully

This chapter explores:

- some principles for getting started
- sequencing the work
- what you'll need
- timelines for re-working time
- pitfalls to watch out for
- how to accelerate progress
- assessing whether your efforts are paying off.

ASK ANY EMPLOYEE about their experience of organizational change and they'll probably wince and show you the scars on their back. Painful, failed change initiatives abound in the corporate world. Even if you've convinced leaders of the benefits of managing time better in your business, how do you work up a successful plan *and* convince the rest of the organization?

Some principles for getting started

Don't be tempted to 'pick and mix' from the time solutions described in Chapters 7 and 8 as a quick fix. A piecemeal approach won't help you to genuinely transform the way people work. Your strategy needs to be guided by your business context and goals, and by your colleagues who will be the 'receivers' of this change.

First, your business context. You're not solving time for time's sake; this is about achieving your strategic and organizational goals. By framing this as a leadership issue, leaders can confidently articulate what the current impact on the business is and why it's imperative to act. It might be about transforming your service to clients; improving your ability to bring new products to market; finding the right hybrid working model for the future; or creating a more gender-inclusive and racially balanced workforce.

Second, your colleagues. A plethora of change initiatives hit the buffers because they've been designed to the nth degree by a central team who are exclusively seeing the business from their own perspective. Project 'push' fails as an approach because it forces a pre-determined solution onto an unwilling audience. There is a better way.

For these two reasons, this book doesn't offer you an off-the-shelf strategy. What it does offer are some principles for creating a strategy that is tailored to *your* business's needs, along with timelines and advice to guide your planning.

These principles will guide your own time strategy:

1. *Find the hook.* Identify the pressing business issue or opportunity that people are keen to resolve or pursue, and describe how managing time differently can help you to achieve this.
2. *Make it leader led and employee owned.* Leaders articulate the desired outcomes – the 'what' – and some broad

principles to guide the effort. Employees figure out the detail and the 'how' to get there.

3. *Make it about how the work gets done.* Ditch ideas of a branded cultural change programme. This should be about meaningful work on specific changes that relate to people's day-to-day activity.

4. *Enable, don't prescribe.* The ongoing role of leaders is to figure out how to support and constructively challenge employees, free up obstacles and smooth the way.

5. *Make good use of time!* Don't add another initiative that drains time and energy and isn't seen as a priority. Give people a better experience of managing time at work *in the way you implement this.*

6. *Be bold and brief.* To get people thinking differently, target a pay-off that warrants a different kind of investment. Incremental tweaks won't help you re-work time meaningfully.

7. *Lean on people who 'get it'.* Give responsibility and visibility to the people who are energized to make this happen; they will be leading the new ways of working.

Sequencing the work

What should the work consist of? What do you address in the early stages and what do you tackle later? The first step is to define the benefits of why you're undertaking this change. This should be aspirational and forward-looking, and articulate clearly where you're going and why. Forget dry language and jargon: you're looking to make this visceral – you want to engage people emotionally as well as rationally. Along with clarity of purpose, you'll need to put some firm stakes in the ground to guide people. These might look like, 'There needs to be a clear business benefit'; 'Simplify, don't overcomplicate'; 'It has to work for the team/ business not just the individual'; 'It has to be equitable for all'.

Once your purpose and guiding stakes are clear, the early stages of the work consist of:

- bringing other leaders on board to form a strong coalition across the business
- appointing a core group to support teams in their re-working efforts
- selecting the first individuals/teams to design the new ways of managing time
- agreeing the first changes to focus on
- conducting pilots, trials and/or experiments
- seeing what works well, replicating successes and learning from failures.

Once you have gained some momentum, the later stages of the work are about:

- adjusting the organization's structure and job designs
- improving work processes, tools and technologies
- updating workplace policies
- looking at implications for pay, benefits, performance management, learning and development.

Let's go back to 'agreeing the first changes to focus on'. How do you know *what* to tackle? Your data gathering, the business case and the traffic light tool will have led you to identify some priorities. Remember to make this about the core work that people do. So choose a pressing business or organizational problem to solve *by using time more effectively*. Give people the freedom to contract with one another differently around their working time. Ask them questions such as:

'How would we do X differently if we collectively made better use of our time at work?'

'If we adopted a longer-term mindset about X, what would that look like in practice?'

'What would be a better way of doing X so that no one is disadvantaged?'

'What would be a more sustainable practice?'

'What can we change today, this year, next year, beyond?'

Share the six traits of time-focused organizations and see what ideas these spark. The point is to trust the people who do the work day in and day out to come up with the answers. If your organization is highly risk-averse, you can appease leaders' nerves by trialling some changes in a smaller business unit or location.

When you're re-working time, don't focus exclusively on tasks and numbers; dig into the emotional consequences too. How do people feel about these changes? What excites them? What are their fears? And there's a personal element to all of this as well as the team or organizational element. What unconscious habits will individuals need to unlearn? What positive behaviours will they need to role model? How can we help people to say 'no' when necessary, or constructively draw attention to unhelpful time practices? Guiding all this work requires some skilled facilitation and the active involvement of leaders, as you'll see shortly.

What you'll need

What does a strategy like this require in terms of resources, skills and budget? The good news is that by avoiding a big branded corporate programme and focusing instead on solving business problems, this is mainly about bringing together the right people and giving them the freedom to think differently. Further down the line, there may be changes required to tools or systems or an increased investment in training, coaching or mentoring programmes. But to complete the early stages of re-working time, you'll need the following:

- a senior sponsor
- a core team

- a trailblazing team
- a re-working process with supporting materials
- access to relevant data
- active involvement of leaders.

The roles should operate as follows:

- *The senior sponsor* should be a strong advocate for managing time better and have clout at the top of the organization. Their role is to protect people as they experiment, help resolve broader issues that they may run into and proactively influence other senior leaders.
- *The core team* orchestrates and supports the re-working activity. They will design the process, facilitate re-working sessions, help people to overcome stumbling blocks, keep momentum up and replicate successes across the organization. Choose participants with the appetite to get involved *and* the right organizational development skills for this kind of work. One core team leader described the skills she needed to draw on: 'My time is spent thinking, collaborating, connecting and helping people understand where we need to get to.'
- *The trailblazing team* may be a cross-business group or from a specific business unit. They are the people tasked with solving a business problem or achieving a target outcome by managing time more effectively. It's important to choose people who 'get' what this is about and see the need for a better way of managing time. Business consultant Gaurav Gupta, co-author with John Kotter of *Change: How Organizations Achieve Hard-to-Imagine Results in Uncertain and Volatile Times*, talks about 'activating people's curiosity' to explore new possibilities.[1] The trailblazing team members should be chosen for their curiosity and energy, and be diverse in terms of demographics and cognitive and thinking styles.
- *The re-working process and materials* describe how your core team will engage with the trailblazing team along with

the information and tools to support them in their work. These may include your timeline, the business case, a description of the outcomes you're looking to achieve, the guiding principles shared by leaders, key messages, agendas for re-working sessions and collaboration tools to help the team develop their proposals.

- *Access to relevant data* is required by the trailblazing team to help them problem-solve or evidence their proposals. These data may be 'owned' by other functions or individuals, so the senior sponsor can help facilitate access to them.
- *Leaders will need to be actively involved* by voicing repeatedly the business reasons *why* a better use of working time is required. They may need to make things uncomfortable by demanding that this is important. They can elevate the story by telling people about what the trailblazers have done, and they can visibly role model the new ways of working and talk positively about these.

Timelines for re-working time

'How long will this take? How quickly can we get going? What should our plan look like?' No doubt these questions are uppermost in your mind at this stage. On the following pages are two sample timelines setting out the steps for re-working time. They aim to provide a starting point for you to tailor as necessary. They assume that you have secured the firm commitment of your leadership team to re-working time; that you have clearly articulated the outcomes you're seeking to achieve and the priorities you will tackle first; and that you have collectively agreed how big and how urgent a deal this is.

The first timeline (Figure 11.1) shows how you can complete a small-scale, fast-cycle trial, in nine weeks, of some changes that are specific to a particular team or business unit. It's deliberately pacy, dynamic work. It may look tough to achieve, but the risk here is actually that you're too under-ambitious. If you play it safe and proceed cautiously, you'll likely see very little meaningful change as a result. This timeline really challenges you to compress the elapsed time between the important discussions and working sessions, so you keep the momentum up and don't lose sight of the goal as the weeks roll by.

Figure 11.1 Timeline 1: Re-working time in a local team or business unit

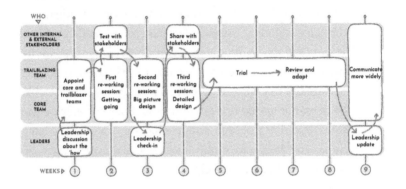

Here's a step-by-step guide to following this first timeline:

1. *Leadership discussion about the 'how'.* Set out your guiding principles and describe the impact you want to achieve over the next nine weeks, or whatever timescale you wish to define.

2. *Appoint core and trailblazer teams.* Move quickly to select the members of the core team who will support this re-working effort and beyond. Identify one or more business teams who are critical to the outcomes you want to achieve.

3. *First re-working session: getting going.* The senior sponsor shares the vision, business case data and the re-working timeline to get people on board and energized. Brainstorm some potential improvements to test with stakeholders.

4. *Test with stakeholders.* Road test your big ideas with the people whose help you need to make this happen.

5. *Second re-working session: big picture design.* Reflect on stakeholders' feedback and work up the proposed changes more thoroughly. What does this mean for different audiences, including 'me'? What would success look like?

6. *Leadership check-in.* Review the big picture design and ask, 'Is this ambitious enough?'; 'Will it get us to where we want to be?'; and 'What does this mean for us individually and collectively as leaders?' How do *you* need to support this change?

7. *Share with stakeholders.* Share the outputs from the leadership check-in and get stakeholders' input to the next two steps.

8. *Third re-working session: detailed design.* Work up the detailed process, materials, messaging and measurement that you need in order to conduct the trial.

9. *Trial.* Put your re-working plan into practice. Be open to continuously evolving it during the trial period.

10. *Review and adapt.* Alongside your trial, gather feedback and run diagnostics to see how well the changes are being received and what impact they are having. What's worked well and less well? How will you incorporate that learning next time?

11. *Leadership update.* Share the trial results, agree how you will share this with the wider organization and then plan from here.

12. *Communicate more widely.* Publicize stories about what the team has achieved to create awareness and demand. Explain the forward plan and how others can get involved.

Timeline 2 (Figure 11.2) shows how you build on this initial stage of local re-working to create a bigger movement encompassing the wider organization. The second wave of trials should involve more teams, and ideally experiment with some cross-business changes. These may take longer to set up and run. Once the trials have reached critical mass and people are adapting successfully to new processes, behaviours, roles and/or tools, then you can start embedding the changes to sustain them over the longer term. At this point, they become 'the way we do things around here'. We'll look at 'embedding' in more detail in the next chapter; essentially, it involves adjusting routines, regular operating processes and people-management programmes so these fully support your new ways of working.

Figure 11.2 Timeline 2: Creating an organization-wide movement

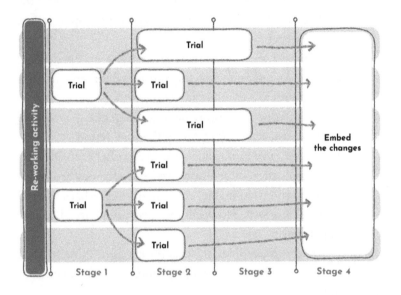

There needs to be a parallel effort to continuously communicate with people about what is going on. In Stage 1, your aim is to build awareness of the 'what' and the 'why'; by Stage 2, you're looking to generate interest and excitement as people start to hear about the early benefits of managing time differently. By sharing stories about what you're seeing and learning, you will stimulate people's curiosity to get involved. As you embark on Stage 3, keep recruiting those who 'get it' and are passionate about playing a role in growing this movement. Your aim is not to control things rigidly from the corporate centre, but to encourage the movement to expand while keeping it true to your original goals and guiding principles. By Stage 4, it should be creating value for your business, generating some notable improvements in productivity and fostering healthier, more inclusive working practices.

Again, this timeline deliberately doesn't specify timings for each stage. These will vary according to the business outcomes you're looking to achieve, the size of your organization and the shift in experience you want to create for employees, clients and external partners. But as a rough guide, for a large multi-site organization Stage 1 could be achieved in nine weeks, Stages 2 and 3 (combined) in nine to 12 weeks and Stage 4 could take between six months and a year.

Pitfalls to watch out for

Bringing about change in an organization is rarely easy; we often end up side-tracked or falling short of our goals. Why? In a nutshell, it is down to human nature. Successfully changing the way people work requires a deep understanding of human mindsets and dynamics, and an ability to influence these thoughtfully – skills that are often overlooked in promotions and senior appointments. In recent research, only 28% of managers felt senior managers in their organization were managing change well.[2] Here are some common pitfalls you may encounter:

- lacking a compelling reason for change
- describing the 'why' in a way that makes intellectual sense but doesn't engage people's emotions
- too few people who are passionate about finding better ways to work
- people feeling like this is being 'done' to them
- making the process of changing so arduous and painful people revert to the status quo

- launching with a big bang and flurry of activity which peters out when the next new thing comes along
- underestimating the time it takes to get people to change their behaviour
- heaping more work or responsibilities on top of people without taking anything away.

You can avoid these pitfalls by painting in tangible terms the change you want to bring about and linking this to the things people care deeply about. Help people to see 'what's in it for me' and build their confidence by appointing credible people to lead the re-working effort. Bring managers with you by involving them in the re-working process, and draw on – or bring in – people with expertise in managing complex organizational changes to help manage the process. The pain of organizational change can be lessened by challenging expectations about how quickly you can move, but it's still essential to plan interventions over a sustained period of time to prevent your progress from stalling or slipping backward. Last but not least, ask what you can *stop* doing in order to manage time better. Productivity is about choosing carefully what you will do and what you *won't* do, then finding the most efficient ways to work. The resources in Appendix 4 include tools and exercises for helping people to identify better ways of managing time; one of these is the 'Stop, Start, Continue' tool, which I have used in many organizations and always found to be effective.

In terms of linking the change to the things people care deeply about, what are these? Some typical answers are: security; fairness; purpose and meaning; control; advancement; growth; compassion; trust; and rewarding relationships in and outside of work. The answer may vary by age or personal situation, but if you've taken time to assess your data through a diversity lens, you'll have a good sense of what different groups care most about.

How to accelerate progress

As well as the pitfalls, there are also opportunities to make tangible progress and signal this to the wider organization. First and foremost, to create momentum it is essential to put re-working time at the heart of your business – it shouldn't happen in a vacuum. After all, it's about finding the optimum way of working for your business that will help you achieve your goals and enable people to flourish. So link your efforts directly with business priorities and any other changes or external drivers, and make it about your clients too: how will your new way of managing time help you better meet *their* needs?

If your new way of managing time is to appeal to – and work fairly for – everyone, it can't be designed by a homogeneous few. Tap into collective intelligence by bringing in under-represented perspectives to contribute and road-test ideas, spot the holes that no one is seeing and ask the awkward questions that no one is voicing. It might feel harder, but it'll get you to a better solution. Equally, this isn't a time for telling people what the answer is but rather for letting people shape the answer. People need to ask questions, have their say, feel listened to *and* feel trusted. By giving them responsibility for designing the detail, they're more likely to get onboard than dig their heels in or head for the door. In cognitive psychology, 'levels of processing' means that when we are more actively involved, we process that learning at a deeper level and it becomes more strongly encoded in our memory. So by trusting people to come up with the answers, you're also building greater change capability.

For example, one insurance company successfully re-worked time in their claims-handling department. Call volumes were typically high on Mondays, with all the car crashes that had happened over the weekend. By Friday, things were pretty quiet. So the company asked the claims handlers, 'How could you do this in a different way?' They invited them to restructure their time so they could get all the work done without it overwhelming them *provided they maintained or exceeded levels of customer service.* The team implemented longer days on Mondays and Tuesdays where people could choose to work two 10-hour days and then take Friday off. Both customer service and morale went up.

As we saw in Chapter 6, managers play a critical role in retaining and motivating team members but are often under-supported during times of change. So involve managers in re-working sessions; give them the tools and autonomy to trial new ideas and don't evaluate their performance negatively if these don't all succeed. You can build in peer support by bringing different managers together to share problems and exchange learning. If you want people to buy into a new way of working, your communications will need to speak to the head *and* heart, and take into account people's differing preferences for the way they process information. You can do this by combining visual, written and aural updates that tell the personal stories as well as the facts. Some people will want the big picture, headlines and conclusions; others will need to see the detail and the step-by-step rationale.

Finally, pick some symbolic acts (not words) that tangibly demonstrate your intent and as you gain momentum, activate people's natural curiosity and overcome the sceptics by promoting these successes widely. And those trailblazers who have led the re-working effort? Appoint them into key roles and give them management responsibility; this will clearly signal the career rewards that are on offer for those who lead your new ways of working.

Assessing whether your efforts are paying off

To help you assess your progress towards your goals and build wider confidence in your new approach to managing time, you'll need an appropriate bundle of metrics. In the past, I've seen intricate measurement strategies and cascading sets of metrics; these might have their place, but they are not easy to communicate and you risk getting lost amidst the detail. For your time strategy, you need a small number of leading and lagging indicators that will quickly and easily tell you how you're doing. They should answer a few important questions, such as, 'What are we seeing and hearing? What's gaining traction and what's not? Why? What's the impact?'

With metrics, it's easy to fall into the trap of relying on 'input' or 'process' measures – for example, the number of re-working sessions held, the quantity of re-working proposals that have been green-lighted, or the latest milestone to be achieved in your time strategy. These tend to be easier to measure than the one question you really want the answer to: is it all making a positive difference? To find this out, your metrics should be outcome focused, even if they're slightly more challenging to measure. They're likely to be a mix of specific business or organizational metrics and some metrics about the employee, client or external partners' experience. Figure 11.3 offers some examples.

Figure 11.3 Example metrics of positive progress

Business and organizational metrics	Experience-based metrics
Higher levels of collective productivity	Higher self-reported levels of wellbeing
New products launched	Fewer stress-related absences
Break-through thinking	People switching off during leave
Higher success rates in competitive contracts	Greater confidence in leaders and managers
Services adapted in response to a crisis	Higher levels of engagement and job satisfaction
Costs and inefficiencies reduced	Higher levels of individual productivity
Improved client feedback and retention rates	Employees feel more connected to colleagues
Merger integrations completed successfully	Greater pride in employer
More senior female and minority ethnic promotions	Fewer experiences of bias, discrimination and micro-aggressions
New career paths established	It feels safer for people to 'be themselves' at work
More diverse intakes	People feel more supported in their careers
More gender-balanced teams at every level	

Many of the above are longer-term outcomes, so do look to include some shorter-term measures too. You can run some simple diagnostics at the start of your re-working activity and then re-run them in the middle and/or at the end of your interventions. Again, these can be both business- and experience-related metrics – for example, improving the quality of client proposals, achieving more diverse interview panels or chairing more productive meetings. Alternatively, look back at your traffic light framework from Chapter 10, if you used this tool. Have any of your red or amber lights changed? Where are you seeing the progress?

Sustaining your progress over time

With any change effort, there's always a risk that people will slide back into old habits or create workarounds that undo some (or all) of the progress you've made. At a certain point, your conscious re-working efforts need to morph into 'business as usual'. How do you hand over responsibility for continuously improving the way you manage working time? The core team doesn't continue for ever, so who does this and how? Plus, the world doesn't stay still so how do you keep your new way of managing time up to date and fit for purpose?

In the final chapter, we'll learn how to embed your progress firmly into your day-to-day operations so your positive time practices become 'the way we do things around here'. You'll discover how to celebrate and share successes and be introduced to a toolkit of resources to help you and your organization stay on track as you lead your business into the future. And we'll take a look at some broader developments that could help us to transform our world of work on a far bigger scale.

Chapter 12
Time after time

How to make time strategies stick, in your organization and beyond

This chapter explores:

- keeping time
- staying on track – expertly evolving
- scaling up
- looking back, looking forward.

IF YOU DON'T want your efforts to re-work time to be consigned to the heap of failed organizational initiatives, you'll need to fully bed down the changes you have introduced. Different people will play important roles in promoting and reinforcing these new working practices and you can capitalize on early wins by publicizing and promoting their benefits. All these things will help you to embed your positive time practices firmly into your organization. By this point, you should be starting to reap some early rewards from your re-working activity and seeing some of the leading indicators start to shift in the right direction.

So can you tick the re-work time box, sit back and relax? Move on to other pressing matters? No – this isn't a case of 'fixed then done'. As the world evolves, the way you manage working time needs to keep pace. This is where the sixth and final trait of time-focused organizations, *expertly evolving*, comes in. How do you actively maintain a growth mindset and make sure your approach to managing time remains fit for purpose? This chapter introduces you to a practical toolkit to help you and your colleagues stay on track over the coming years, and looks beyond your organization's boundaries at how we can bring about lasting change across a far bigger sphere.

First, let's look at how to make your own time strategy stick.

Keeping time

In Chapter 6, we saw how a *deliberately designed* organization ensures *all* of its operating model helps people focus on the important work. Remember that metaphor from Chapter 10 of the organization as a fleet of ships? You've tackled the headline changes and lined up the fleet forerunners – they are steaming ahead with gusto. Now you need to bring the rest of the fleet into line to help you achieve your goals – in other words, to reinforce your new way of managing time.

Your people management policies and processes take centre stage here: recruitment, performance management, promotions, pay, benefits, resourcing, talent management, learning and development. If you're still setting time-based objectives instead of outcome-oriented goals, people won't change their behaviours. If pay progression is based on time served instead of the value people have created for the business, you won't incentivize more productive ways of working or eliminate an important barrier to equality in the workplace.

You'll also need to review your established leadership and management practices. How could you update your leadership behaviours and development programmes, and how you spend your time as a leadership team? Look carefully at 'amateur' managers:[1] can you professionalize their managerial skills? Appoint managers who demonstrate high-quality management skills, including how well they manage their team's working time. Other operational routines and systems will need to be re-evaluated too, such as your business planning and review cycles, your IT systems and tools, and how you share knowledge and conduct meetings. Instead of routinely taking up hours of people's time in a bureaucratic numbers-driven exercise, business planning and review cycles could be focused more sharply on the outcomes you're looking to achieve and draw on people's time differently. Why not replace the big annual or semi-annual exercise with smaller, more frequent, locally controlled discussions – in some parts of the business at least – about progress towards goals and the in-year readjustment of financial and other resources? This is similar in concept to the way performance management processes are evolving, as we saw in Chapter 8. Look, too, at the gender and ethnic composition of those controlling the financial planning process and decisions; if they are very homogeneous, might it benefit the business more to bring in other perspectives? With IT tools and systems, Chapter 7 suggested how to choose and use technology better from a time-management perspective, from being more selective with the amount of self-service tools pushed onto employees to using tools that are designed and deployed with cognitive wellbeing as a priority.

Reinforcing roles

You might be thinking, 'What can you do if you're not the CEO?' Everyone has their part to play; here's how leaders, managers, HR professionals, team members and clients can support your new approach to managing time:

- *Leaders* can role model time-intelligent leadership behaviours and coach others. They can call out unhelpful practices that squander people's time or exclude certain individuals.

- *Line managers* can explore different ways of working and guide their teams in developing new time contracts. By understanding their own biases and preferences, they can be more conscious of their personal impact on others.
- *Individual employees* can help agree a healthier, more productive way of working across the team, adopt good time management habits and be mindful of their own and others' boundaries around working time.
- *Activists* quickly see the potential to work in better ways and promote positive change. They speak up publicly, surface resistance when they encounter it and advocate on behalf of others.
- *Whistleblowers* flag up persistently unhelpful practices that are damaging to people and the organization over the longer term. If your environment doesn't encourage people to talk openly about these instances, people need a safe way of being heard.
- *HR, OD, diversity, inclusion and wellbeing professionals* can propose changes that get to the very heart of the way work is managed, improve the quality of workforce data and collect valuable data about employees' experiences too.
- Finally, *clients and external partners* can be open to new modes of service delivery by not demanding 24/7 availability from individuals, accepting delegation and respecting new working patterns. They can be a force for good by pushing their advisers and service providers to adopt ways of working that encourage diversity and promote cognitive and mental wellbeing.

Celebrating and sharing successes

When you're changing the way your organization operates and asking people to do things differently, positive reinforcements and rewards are vital to signal the momentum you're gaining and build people's confidence. Publicize progress via informal and formal channels, with leaders playing an influential role by sharing stories and anecdotes about these achievements.

If you're wondering what success might look like when you've re-worked time, here are eight examples of differing scale and complexity, together with a proposal for how you might publicize each achievement.

1. Try a new way of resourcing and delivering a project that develops junior team members and frees up project leaders' time to manage, not 'do'. Gather positive client feedback and share this with the team and business leaders.

2. Review how time was invested in recent competitive tenders and identify better ways of using this time to increase future successes. Formalize your improvements into standard guidance for all teams and apply these to some high-profile opportunities.

3. Introduce a 'triage' process for fast-tracking decisions on whether to pursue new leads or responding to requests for additional work. Share examples of how quickly a cross-business team has been mobilized to pursue the lead or resource the work.

4. Invite contributors into major decision-making meetings in person rather than commissioning papers. Describe how the quality of discussion, decision-making and subsequent outcomes have improved as a result.

5. Invite different colleagues in turn to chair part or all of regular meetings. Share one piece of positive feedback about each person's chairing style and encourage colleagues to lead a more senior internal or client-facing meeting.

6. Develop new late-stage career paths and hybrid roles for colleagues approaching retirement. Share these during the recruitment process to show the variety of career paths

available and explain how these new roles are enhancing profitability, retention and transfer of learning.

7. Trial new ways of bringing colleagues back from extended leave, slowly ramping up working time in the office and/ or remotely. Invite returners to describe their experiences and the benefits at employee network events, in blogs and interviews and in wellbeing programmes.

8. Test new business ideas on school leavers and undergraduates as part of your early career outreach. Form a regular feature or prize, and highlight successful responses in early careers materials and corporate literature.

Staying on track – *expertly evolving*

This sixth trait of time-focused organizations describes a constant attitude of curiosity, creativity and perseverance about the way they value and manage working time. Professor Carol Dweck articulates a growth mindset as, 'The passion for stretching yourself and sticking to it, even (and especially) when it's not going well… This is the mindset that allows people to thrive in challenging times.'[2] It's not just people that thrive as a result; businesses do too. By developing greater adaptability, wellbeing and resilience in your workforce, your business can respond more easily and effectively to changing circumstances. Professor Dweck's research confirms that, 'By spending a small fraction of their overall investment in preparing people to embrace the future as a world of possibility, businesses can accelerate and de-risk their future of work programmes.'[3]

#24 Instil a growth mindset about how you manage time at work

This final time solution helps you to maintain and adapt your new time culture successfully over the months and years ahead, long after the dust has settled on your initial change efforts. Chapter 6 set out how *expertly evolving* organizations do four things really well: they experiment and learn; they keep a collectively open mind; they encourage resourcefulness through coaching practices; and they build long-term time management capability.

With *experimenting and learning*, this can feel really hard to do in risk-averse organizations or businesses that are always chasing the numbers. It's daunting if you're swimming against the tide or sticking your head above the parapet. The answer is to band together – focus on what's in your team's sphere of control, trial some changes and ask for forgiveness later when you're hopefully trumpeting your successes.

Keeping a collectively open mind means regularly looking at your organizational and business data and asking, 'What are we not paying attention to? Where are our blind spots? What different perspectives can we bring in?' Likewise, as individuals and as teams, we can reflect frequently on our time habits and identify where these are no longer fit for purpose.

Encouraging resourcefulness focuses on leaders' and managers' roles as coaches. They can invite others to be curious and creative about work habits and outcomes – successful or otherwise – by asking questions like, 'What are we finding difficult here? Who or what can we lean on for help? What can we draw from these setbacks? What was it that helped us to achieve a positive impact?'

Businesses invest millions in building the technical and transferable skills they need for their organization to perform successfully today and in the future, so why wouldn't you invest in building *long-term capability in managing working time* too? This has the potential to become an organizational strength and an enviable source of competitive advantage.

Developing a growth mindset in time management needn't mean adding to our workload. Instead, it's about recognizing when our existing mental models and work habits need updating because they no longer serve our goals. And it's about believing we have the potential to find or create better ways of working together, instead of thinking we already have all the answers or that our organizations always have to operate the way they do today. Appendix 4 contains a complete toolkit of resources to help you put a growth mindset into practice as a leader, manager or individual. Many of its tools can help you achieve other organizational or business goals too.

In addition to the toolkit, you'll find three further resources in the Appendices to help you engage and brainstorm with others about re-working time in your organization:

1. a brief synopsis of this book's central messages
2. 30 arguments for re-working time (10 each on boosting productivity, diversity and wellbeing)
3. a time solution library listing all 24 time solutions described in Parts 2 and 3.

Re-working time is a pervasive concept – it informs many organization development and human resources practices. It can help to unify and enhance the various improvements on which you are already working in your businesses. So consider the concepts and practices described in this book and identify how you can usefully draw on these to complement your existing initiatives.

Now let's widen our perspective once again to look beyond your organization's boundaries at the bigger picture.

Scaling up

It's encouraging to see companies such as KBC Group and Zurich Insurance Group strive to create healthier, more productive workplaces, contribute positively to society and reduce their impact on the environment. But not every business is persuaded to think beyond the narrow and often short-term financial goals that serve the primary interests of their shareholders and owners. How do we move beyond changing organizations one at a time to achieve a transformative shift in society that will benefit future generations? How do we change public policies and politics to help create a healthier, more productive work culture, nation by nation, that generates real value for businesses as well as for individuals?

There are broader efforts underway with these aspirations in their sights. In the United Kingdom, the Good Business Foundation launched the Good Business Charter[4] in February 2020. This invites organizations in the United Kingdom to gain accreditation for responsible business practices, including fairer hours and contracts, employee wellbeing, employee representation, and diversity and inclusion. There are regional efforts as well – for example, in London the Good Work Standard launched by the Mayor of London sets out a benchmark for 'best employment practices' above legal requirements and bestows two levels of certification.

Then there are the international campaigns. One international cohort of politicians, social leaders and business experts is calling on governments to shorten the working week without reducing pay,[5] whilst the burgeoning B Corps movement[6] is a global community of leaders promoting 'a new kind of business that balances purpose and profit'. Businesses that have gained B Corp accreditation have committed to higher levels of transparency and legal accountability for their social and environmental performance. Over 74 countries and 150 industries are involved to date and in the United Kingdom there are currently 430 B Corps with a combined revenue in excess of £4.3 billion and over 22,000 employees.

A global movement can achieve impressive results, but often legislation needs updating to better reflect the realities of modern working lives and to adjust the imbalance of power between employer and employee. With greater job protection and security, for example, employees may feel less compelled to work all hours in competitive professions simply to hold onto a job that pays the bills.

In the United Kingdom, the proposed *Better Business Act* would require every company to give equal consideration to the interests of all stakeholders, not just their shareholders.[7] If enacted, via an amendment to Section 172 of the *Companies Act 2006*, it would no longer be optional for directors to 'align the long-term interests of people, planet and profit'. It would switch off the default position of 'shareholder primacy' for all companies and empower business leaders and owners to operate in a way that benefits employees, society *and* the natural environment.

By updating legislative and regulatory frameworks and offering positive policy incentives, governments can make our nations attractive places for businesses to locate to or expand in. By investing in their businesses there, companies can signal loudly and clearly that they care about job sustainability, environmental sustainability and healthy work lives that encourage individuals and families to flourish. Where there are good-quality jobs that don't squash employees' potential or overwhelm their lives, talented people will follow and, over time, greater economic prosperity will ensue. Governments are waking up to this: Spain, Sweden, Ireland and Iceland are currently trialling shorter working weeks; New Zealand and Scotland are advocating likewise. It may be a case of the public sector leading the way, with the private sector jumping on the bandwagon when the benefits are clearly demonstrated.

Looking back, looking forward

In this chapter, we've learnt how embedding your new time practices in the day-to-day workings of your organization can prevent your progress from stalling or grinding to a halt.

We've understood how *expertly evolving* organizations remain open and attentive to how they manage working time, to chart their course through an ever-changing and unpredictable environment.

And we've reflected on the broader developments that could boost our ambitions to re-work time on a far wider scale.

While these campaigns and pieces of legislation are admirable in their intent, there is scant evidence that they have had any impact on our time culture so far. The statistics on overwork, ill-health, poor productivity and limited diversity from Part 1 still stand out in stark relief. Perplexingly, organizations can be signed up to many benchmarks and awarded the highest levels of accreditation, *yet still operate with complete time blindness*. The actual experiences of employees aren't materially changing in any significant way because our time culture is so relentlessly ignored. We simply can't afford to sit back and wait for the next charter or new legislation – we've got to shift the needle *now*.

There's one last question for you and your business to consider, which we explore in the Conclusion.

One-minute summary of Part 3

1. The first steps in re-working time are to:
   - understand what your current approach is
   - assess how well this is working for your business and how it is impacting employees
   - secure leaders' active support.
2. You're not solving time for time's sake.
3. Your time strategy should be:
   - tailored to your strategic and organizational goals
   - about meaningful changes to day-to-day work
   - leader-led and employee-owned.
4. Fast-cycle, dynamic trials can be rolled out progressively.
5. Early progress in re-working time needs to be reinforced by your people management policies and processes, and your leadership practices.
6. Everyone has their part to play in adopting your new approach to managing time, but their roles will vary.
7. Businesses can develop a growth mindset and long-term capability in managing working time well to help them continuously adapt to an ever-changing environment.
8. There are active campaigns, public policies and legislative proposals aimed at creating more sustainable, productive businesses… yet our time culture remains broken.

Conclusion

One today is worth two tomorrows. Lost time is never found again. Time is money. Dost thou love life? Then do not squander time, for that's the stuff that life is made of. You may delay, but time will not.

Benjamin Franklin

THE FINAL QUESTION for us each to reflect on is, 'What do we want to be known and remembered for?' For accepting a business culture that never stops for breath and squanders its seemingly infinite access to human resources? What will we say to the next generation when, as with climate change, they turn to us and ask, 'What did *you* do to help make working lives more sustainable, to value resources more thoughtfully, to create a better future for those of us who follow?'

It's up to us

If your sole measures of business success are about growth and financial rewards, then you're unlikely to heed this book's message. It's likely that in material terms at least, sticking with the status quo is going to be more rewarding in your eyes (but if you've read this far, perhaps you're thinking again). Will you still feel that way at the end of your career when you look back and ponder on what might have been?

If you accept that our current attitude to time at work is unhealthy, unproductive and unfair for many, but you're thinking, 'We'll never really crack this. It's too hard, too complex, too ambitious', then I urge you to think again.

If there's a voice in your head saying, 'There is a better way to build our businesses, to nurture people's careers, to bring different people together and achieve great things', then now is the time to stop and listen to it.

By many measures, we are at a turning point in our history. We have a once-in-a-lifetime chance to reconsider how we work day by day, month by month. We teeter on the cusp of a new possibility for reshaping our societies, our way of living, our relationship with the natural world and our world of work. Imagine a point in our future when, all around us, we witness the ways of working described in this book. Picture for a moment the possibilities and the powerful potential for individuals, for labour markets, for the clients and communities that our businesses serve.

What will our role be in bringing this about? Will we be bystanders, waiting and hoping for others to take the lead? Or will we be courageous and step forward to do what we can in our own roles, in our own workplaces and in our own ways to create healthier, more productive organizations? If so, then one day we may look back at this moment and say yes, that was when we embraced the future of time.

Appendices

Appendix 1:
The book in brief

THE WAY WE think about and manage time at work is broken. We typically think about time management only in relation to the individual, and our cultural norms about time at work emphasize speed, urgency, 24/7 availability and a short-term focus.

This time culture is deeply ingrained into the way our organizations are designed and operate – we rarely stop to think about it or question it. This 'time blindness' causes organizational defects that damage our productivity, wellbeing and diversity:

- *Productivity*: because in our cult of busyness and fragmentation of work time we've lost sight of how to productively focus on the priorities.
- *Wellbeing*: because jobs and careers feel unsustainable for many causing high stress levels and burnout and negatively affecting interpersonal relationships.
- *Diversity*: because there are winners and losers in this time culture. Winners can 'give what it takes' to get ahead; those who can't are disadvantaged.

External pressures and our outdated mindset about time are twin challenges to which businesses urgently need to respond. How?

We need to fix the system, not the individual. We do this by treating working time as a strategic asset and managing it in a collective, thoughtful way.

Time-focused organizations that value and manage time successfully have six traits:

1. *They are outcome-oriented.* They focus on outcomes and leaders role model 'time intelligence'.
2. *They are deliberately designed.* They minimize distractions and help people to focus on the important work.
3. *They are actively aware.* They foster healthy collective habits and environments.
4. *They are career committed.* They promote long-term careers and offer tailored 'time deals'.
5. *They are community cultivators.* They value humanity, social cohesion and wellbeing.
6. *They are expertly evolving.* They prize experimentation, learning and open-mindedness and build long-term time management capability.

The Future of Time sets out 24 time solutions – positive practices that can help your organization manage and value time better. Drawing on organization development theory, these solutions span governance, leadership, organization design, processes and technology, people management, environment, behaviours, working patterns and more.

Your strategy for re-working time should be tailored to your business's needs and priorities, and be centred on the core work that people do. You're not solving time for time's sake but in order to achieve your strategic and organizational goals.

Your business will benefit from re-working time by (1) closing diversity gaps; (2) increasing workforce flexibility; (3) maintaining competitive advantage; (4) rebounding faster in response to critical events; and (5) outperforming over the longer term.

Appendix 2:
Thirty arguments for
re-working time

Re-working time boosts productivity by:

1. making strategic decisions about how work effort is invested
2. enabling better quality and more timely decision-making
3. allowing people to focus on the important work and do this efficiently
4. minimizing wasted time through streamlining and simplifying work
5. designing operating models that are nimble and adaptable to changing needs
6. striking a balance between urgent vs important, and immediate vs the longer term
7. fostering a time-aware mindset at organizational, team and individual levels

8. creating physical and virtual environments where people can do their best work
9. enabling businesses to match skilled resources to areas of high demand
10. drawing on collective intelligence internally and externally.

Re-working time boosts diversity by:

1. creating a culture that genuinely values different experiences and perspectives
2. enabling minority employees to be heard and listened to
3. helping minority employees create stronger professional networks
4. ensuring equal access to sought-after work opportunities regardless of background
5. reducing bias in people management decisions
6. broadening the talent pool that employers can access
7. improving retention with flexible, creative career paths
8. encouraging creativity, collaboration and continuous learning
9. offering employees flexibility, value and control through time-centric policies and benefits
10. decreasing the risk of minority employees feeling excluded and leaving.

Re-working time boosts wellbeing by:

1. reducing cognitive depletion and enhancing mental acuity
2. promoting time-intelligent behaviours and healthy time habits
3. forging social bonds and strong communities
4. encouraging listening, empathy and kindness so people feel accepted and valued

5. building resilience to cope – individually and collectively – with setbacks and change
6. creating psychologically safe organizations where people feel able to speak up
7. optimizing individual and collective energy levels
8. improving relationships between managers and team members
9. designing more sustainable workloads and work lives
10. reducing stress, anxiety and burnout by addressing time poverty and pressure.

Appendix 3:
Time solutions library

Below is a list of all 24 positive time practices mentioned in this book.

Appendix 4: Toolkit for re-working time

THIS TOOLKIT CAN help you establish a growth mindset around managing and valuing time strategically in your own work life, as a team and as an organization.

- *Tool 1: Sample team time contract.* This is an illustrative team time contract to kickstart your own discussions as a team about how you can work more productively and ensure that every individual feels heard, and that they are able to contribute and grow professionally.
- *Tool 2: Time awareness training agenda.* These two suggested agendas for training sessions can help you raise awareness about collective time management and build skills and expertise in it.
- *Tool 3: Checklist for individuals.* This checklist offers prompts to guide you in reflecting on your *personal* time choices and habits. By stepping back from the detail of our day jobs, we can become more aware of unconscious patterns into which we've fallen and make more thoughtful decisions

about how we invest our own valuable time at work (and home).

- *Tool 4: Team exercises.* This is not one tool, but eight tried-and-tested techniques for enhancing your team's effectiveness in multiple ways, from prioritizing to problem-solving, and from visioning to reviewing. They'll get your team thinking differently and help you to collectively manage your time better.

- *Tool 5: Checklist for managers.* Being a successful manager requires specific people and organizational skills, not just technical expertise (being good at the day job). Managing time successfully across the team or unit requires a manager to be aware of their *own* time habits and choices, and how these impact the team's productivity, wellbeing and diversity; this checklist helps managers to do exactly that.

- *Tool 6: Team check-in.* You may be familiar with the four stages of team development identified by Bruce Tuckman[1] in the mid-1960s: forming, storming, norming and performing. The key point of his model is that your team's stage of development is never fixed but always evolving. Similarly, the way you're managing time as a team now will evolve as well, with or without conscious intention. So check in with the team on a regular basis regarding how effectively you are working together and what you might need to be paying more attention to.

Tool 1: Sample team time contract

How to use this tool

Start the discussion by recapping the business outcomes you want to achieve. Then, some helpful introductory questions are:

1. What are people spending their time on?
2. What's helping people focus on the important work?
3. What's draining energy, causing unnecessary work or excluding some from contributing?

4. What do colleagues need from one another to do their best work?

Highlight the positives and explore how you can build on these in other ways. Acknowledge the frustrations and invite the team to propose a better way of using their working time. Work through the prompts provided in Chapter 7; below is an example of how an agreed Time Contract might look. Obviously the details will vary depending on your business, team composition and other factors.

Figure A4.1 Sample team time contract

- We will be co-located on Mondays and Wednesdays for team meetings, collaborative work and social events.
- Our team's core hours will be 10.00 am to 12.30 pm and 2.00 pm to 4.00 pm. Outside of these times, team members may not be available or respond immediately.
- Our meeting-free windows are 12.30 to 1.30 pm daily, and Friday afternoons.
- We aim to acknowledge/send an initial response to emails within the following timeframes:
  - the same working day for client emails and urgent internal emails
  - within 24 hours for non-urgent internal emails.
- We'll prioritize meetings for days when we are physically co-located and 'heads down' work for days when we're working remotely.
- We will hold meetings when we want to brainstorm, make decisions, plan, conduct reviews, celebrate or understand major announcements. We won't hold meetings for routine updates, gathering feedback or sharing information that could be circulated in other ways.
- Our meetings will:
  - invite essential, active contributors only
  - always include an agenda listing specific objectives
  - allow everyone to contribute their view before discussion begins
  - conclude with confirming actions and decisions.

- On every major project/work activity:
  - we'll agree buddy pairs to stand in/share updates when one person is unavailable/absent
  - we'll agree in advance what work will be delegated by senior to junior colleagues and how/when feedback will be given
  - we'll agree and share specific on-the-job learning and development opportunities for every team member
  - we'll hold pre-, mid- and post-mortem reviews on how to make better use of our time and efforts.
- We'll prioritize time for learning and development through:
  - half-hour team learning sessions on a weekly basis
  - a half-day every month for self-directed learning and development
  - quarterly events/talks with internal/external invited speakers.
- People are encouraged to connect socially through:
  - a dedicated virtual channel
  - informal chat for the first five to 10 minutes of every meeting
  - a half-hour team walk at lunchtime when co-located
  - monthly team coffees (virtual or physical).
- We'll signal 'deep working' or thinking time by putting headphones on in the office and our online status to 'do not disturb'. We'll avoid interrupting others during their deep work.
- We'll review this time contract once a quarter.

Tool 2: Time awareness training agenda

How to use this tool

Time awareness training for individuals and teams could start to shift mindsets by asking the following questions:

- When do we do our best work?

- What does a healthy, productive day/week/month/year look like for me?
- What are our time sinks?
- How do my work habits impact other people's working time?
- What practices help/hinder us in making the most of our working time as a team?

The agenda could cover:

1. recognizing helpful and unhelpful norms around time at work
2. exploring individual preferences relating to energy levels and working environments
3. identifying the time habits at work that promote physical and mental wellbeing
4. appreciating the impact of our time choices on others
5. having constructive conversations about how we manage time at work.

Training sessions to build expertise in collectively managing time could cover:

1. sharing the business case for positive time management
2. defining what productivity means at organizational, team and individual levels
3. describing the positive time norms and practices you wish to promote
4. equipping people with the language, tools and examples to help them manage working time well
5. signposting relevant HR, wellbeing and other workplace policies.

These sessions needn't be called 'time management' training sessions if that language doesn't work for your business. They might be about 'working at our best', 'collaborating successfully together' or 'creating healthier work lives'. You could include them in your induction process for new joiners as a valuable way for them to understand 'how things work around here'.

Tool 3: Checklist for individuals

How to use this tool

Pick a time when you're not chasing a deadline or needing to be available for others. Take 10 minutes to read through the list below and note down any observations and ideas that come to mind. Identify one or two actions that you can implement tomorrow or in the coming week, and decide when you'll next review your progress and the checklist. Over time, this small but valuable investment of effort can help you stay on track career-wise and manage your own working time more successfully.

Figure A4.2 Checklist for individuals

Your priorities

1. How do you want to be investing your time? ☐
   Think daily, weekly, monthly and quarterly.

2. What are the rocks in your bucket (aka your priorities)?[2] ☐
   Look at whether you're spending enough time on these.

3. Are you still chasing the important stuff? ☐
   Check in with others regularly about the priorities.

4. Is your work day an undifferentiated stretch of time? ☐
   Plan it proactively to get more done and stop boundaries stretching.

Your energy

5. Are you an owl or lark? ☐
   Manage your energy, not just your time.

6. **What does 'eating the frog' look like for you?** ❏
   Invest your upfront time or peak hours in the big things.

7. **What are you investing precious energy in ignoring?** ❏
   Apply the five-minute rule to accomplish small, distracting actions.

8. **What time buffers can help you cope with your day?** ❏
   Build these into your diary and make them visible.

Your productivity

9. **When do you escape into busyness or procrastination?** ❏
   Spot your best ways of avoiding stressful or unpalatable tasks.

10. **Where can you batch process?** ❏
    Put similar chores together to be more efficient.

11. **What are your time sinks?** ❏
    Know where you're wasting time on low value habits.

12. **How much deep thinking time do you need each week?** ❏
    Block out time for reflection, planning and mind wandering.

Your wellbeing

13. **What's your sleep like (honestly)?** ❏
    Stick to a sleep schedule, even just one or two nights a week.

14. **Are you feeding your brain?** ❏
    Detach from work every 90–120 minutes to aid cognitive functioning.

15. **Does your plan for the day include breaks and exercise?** ❏
    Put them in your schedule however short they are.

16. **Do you relinquish your time easily?** ☐
    Protect your time windows by asking colleagues or
    family to help.

Your relationships

17. **Who are you spending your time with?** ☐
    Check your circle and how you wish to widen it.

18. **What emotional spillovers are intruding from home** ☐
    into work?
    Consider the consequences and whether you're okay
    with these.

19. **What small things can you ask of others?** ☐
    Make your requests confidently. People love to help.

20. **How are you role modelling your positive time** ☐
    habits?
    Reflect on how you signal these to others.

Tool 4: Team exercises

How to use this tool

First up are two ways to clarify your *priorities*.

- *Urgent vs important matrix.* With your team, collate a list
  of all the things on which people are spending time,
  listing each activity or project on a post-it note. On a
  flipchart, draw a large square divided into four quarters.
  The horizontal axis is for importance with 'low' on the
  left, 'high' on the right. The vertical axis is for urgency
  with 'low' at the bottom, 'high' at the top. Plot each post-
  it, encouraging debate and questions. At the end, review
  each quadrant and agree the implications for how you
  individually and collectively spend your time across these
  activities.

- *Team time investment.* Using the same list of activities, invite your team members to estimate how many hours or days they are spending on average per week on each activity. It doesn't need to be precise, just a rough guide. You could look back over the last two weeks or a longer period. Calculate the average hourly or daily employment cost for your team (aim for a fully loaded rate including bonuses and benefits, not just salaries). Then use this rate to work out what your collective time investment in each activity is costing in financial terms. What conclusions do you draw? What return on investment are you seeing?

Next are two failsafe ways to get your team thinking differently. The first draws on past successes; the second anticipates future possibilities. Both techniques can help you *envision* better ways of working.

- *Appreciative enquiry.* Invite your team to describe a time in the past when they did their best work and achieved outstanding results. What did they do? How did this feel? What obstacles did they overcome? Then dig deeper into *the factors that enabled this success.* How did they invest their working time? How did they prioritize, collaborate and make decisions? Draw out the learning from this experience that you can apply to the work you are doing today.

- *Stand in the future.* Ask your team to imagine the date is five years from now and they are journalists from a leading business or industry publication. Their latest article/video/podcast describes the success your team has achieved, the impact they've had and how they have made this happen. Divide people into groups of two or three and ask them to write or record this story. Share the results with one another and identify how you can apply these insights to your work today.

However ambitious your aspirations, teams can become bogged down as tasks are added and processes become over-complicated. The next two exercises describe effective ways of *reviewing* what's eating up your time.

- *Now, nominate, next.* As a team, brainstorm a list of all the activities, meetings, obstacles or issues that are draining your collective time and productivity. Draw up three columns headed 'Now', 'Nominate' and 'Next'. Under 'Now', place all the activities that you can change quickly without needing permission or funding. Under 'Nominate', agree how you can delegate more successfully within or outside the team. Under 'Next', identify those bigger ticket items that you can redesign over the longer term and that may need some budget and approvals.
- *Stop, start, continue.* Using the same starting list as above, create three headings of 'Stop', 'Start' and 'Continue'. Which activities or meetings can you simply stop spending time on? What new and better ways of working can you identify under 'Start'? And what practices are valuable ones to 'Continue', adapting as necessary to make better use of your team's time?

The final two exercises help you to *problem-solve* effectively. The first is a continuous process of reflection and learning between colleagues. The second builds your change agency as a team, encouraging you to use your influence to the full.

- *Co-mentoring.* This is where two colleagues, or a small group, meet regularly to talk about any time management challenges they are facing, goals they are working towards or simply to reflect and think out loud. One participant speaks in turn while the other listens and offers practical advice from their own experiences if this is welcomed. Co-mentoring has some parallels with the practice of action learning developed by Reg Revans in the 1950s and documented by author Mike Pedler in *Action Learning for Managers*;[3] this is widely used for tackling important organizational issues and developing people in the process.

- *Areas of change control.* Draw a large square on a flipchart. The vertical axis describes 'timing', with 'now', 'next month', 'next year' and 'far future' listed in ascending order. The horizontal axis describes 'who', with 'me', 'my team', 'my business area' and 'my organization' listed from left to right. Brainstorm any issues that are draining your team's time and performance, and plot these on the chart. The issues that fall in the bottom left quadrant are within your team's direct area of influence; the remaining issues fall outside of your sphere of control. Focus on what you can do now to resolve those problems over which you have agency. Decide on which of the wider issues you will engage with others, when and how.

Tool 5: Checklist for managers

How to use this tool

As with the checklist for individuals, take 10 minutes on a regular basis to reflect on the questions below and consider your own ways of working. What insights come to mind? How might you test these with others to hear their perspectives?

Figure A4.3 Checklist for managers

PRODUCTIVITY	DIVERSITY	WELLBEING
1. How much time am I spending on routine team processes and meetings? How valuable is this and are there more productive ways of doing this?	1. How equally am I dividing my coaching or one-to-one time across the team?	1. How often am I sending emails or contacting people at late hours or weekends, signalling I'm online and available for work?
2. When did I last check in with the team about our collective priorities and any shifting of effort required?	2. Who am I not putting forward or encouraging for promotion or development opportunities and why?	2. Am I transparently leading by example in switching off, taking breaks and maintaining healthy work habits?
3. Who and what am I rewarding and why? Am I unconsciously favouring those who are more present, speak out more, have been in their role for longer?	3. What assumptions am I making about people's availability, particularly early in the morning or late in the day?	3. Am I visibly acknowledging the value of different kinds of work activities (collaborative, focused, etc.) and environments?
4. Where might I be avoiding tackling poor performance or allowing team members to delegate upwards?	4. What assumptions am I making about someone's workload, preferences or ambitions that I could usefully check with them?	4. What social, informal or team development time am I encouraging and facilitating and how?
5. What are our reward mechanisms reinforcing? What changes might incentivize a more valuable use of time across the team?	5. How much of my time do I spend answering questions, proposing solutions and taking the lead vs listening, enquiring and delegating to team members?	5. What signals am I picking up about team members who may be experiencing time pressure or time poverty?

Tool 6: Team check-in

How to use this tool

At a face-to-face team meeting, explore each of the following aspects of team effectiveness in the order indicated. You can do this in a light-touch way, taking a couple of minutes for each, or do a deeper dive by investing an hour of reflection and discussion. Invite people to rate the team on each element using a scale of 1–10 where 1 is low and 10 is high. Encourage people to share their views; don't judge their responses, just listen and acknowledge. Afterwards decide as a team what observations, ideas or issues you want to work further, either now or later, and agree how you'll do this.

Figure A4.4 Team check-in tool

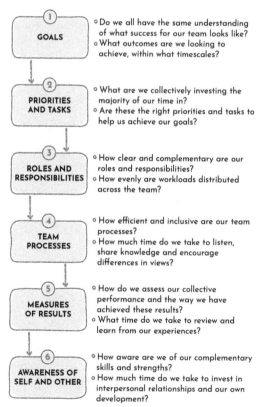

1. **GOALS**
   - Do we all have the same understanding of what success for our team looks like?
   - What outcomes are we looking to achieve, within what timescales?

2. **PRIORITIES AND TASKS**
   - What are we collectively investing the majority of our time in?
   - Are these the right priorities and tasks to help us achieve our goals?

3. **ROLES AND RESPONSIBILITIES**
   - How clear and complementary are our roles and responsibilities?
   - How evenly are workloads distributed across the team?

4. **TEAM PROCESSES**
   - How efficient and inclusive are our team processes?
   - How much time do we take to listen, share knowledge and encourage differences in views?

5. **MEASURES OF RESULTS**
   - How do we assess our collective performance and the way we have achieved these results?
   - What time do we take to review and learn from our experiences?

6. **AWARENESS OF SELF AND OTHER**
   - How aware are we of our complementary skills and strengths?
   - How much time do we take to invest in interpersonal relationships and our own development?

About the author

Helen Beedham, MA Cantab, writes, speaks and advises clients on how to create more inclusive, productive workplaces where everyone can flourish. For the past 25 years, as management consultant then chair of a City-wide professional network, she has led change programmes for FTSE 100 businesses and regularly brought together heads of HR, diversity, inclusion and wellbeing to exchange market-leading practices. She delivers talks for employers; conducts research and publishes articles on organizational and career topics; and speaks at conferences, industry panels and client events. She has interviewed and podcasted with MPs, board members, CEOs, authors and workplace experts, and been cited in the national and HR press. An active mentor, she helped to establish the Women's Network at Trinity College Cambridge and co-steers the United Kingdom's first Workplace Fertility Community. She lives in rural Kent with her husband, daughter and three pet chickens.

www.helenbeedham.com

 @helenbeedham

 helenjbeedham

 @helenjbeedham

Join *The Future of Time* community to keep up with the latest news, discussions and resources for managing time successfully, to help you and your business flourish.

www.community.thefutureoftime.co.uk

-

#thefutureoftime

www.thefutureoftime.co.uk

Acknowledgements

I F IT TAKES a village to raise a child, it takes a whole town to write and launch a book. I may have typed the words onto the page, but a great number of people played a part in bringing this book to life. I'm deeply grateful to all of them.

First, a heartfelt thank you to my publisher, Alison Jones, for spotting the potential in my idea and nurturing it throughout your Business Book Proposal Challenge – which I highly recommend to anyone thinking of writing a business book – and beyond. You've welcomed me into your book community, coached me into my new identity as an author, and patiently answered my numerous questions and dilemmas over the past months. I've loved every bit of this whole book-writing experience. My grateful thanks also go to the wonderful team at Practical Inspiration Publishing, particularly Michelle Charman, Shell Cooper, Susan Jarvis, Frances Staton and Judith Wise; Lizzie Evans, Sarah Rendell and Sophie Robinson from Newgen Publishing UK; and Fiachra McCarthy for designing the book's brilliant cover.

During a year of lockdowns, it was a pleasure and a huge source of practical help to speak with many different people about the ideas and examples in this book. Thank you to the following people for sharing your time, experiences and expertise to help me shape the narrative: Alex Soojung-Kim Pang, Amanda Scott, Anette Bohm,

Camilla Faith, Celia Kirwan, David Henderson, David MacLeod, Gaurav Gupta, Jissille Pillay, John Bruce-Jones, Joris Wonders, Laura Whelan, Lindsay James, Margaret Ruiseal, Matt Nixon, Peter Stonor, Selina-Valencia McDonald, Stuart Turnbull, Susan Heinlein and Zelda Kay, plus others who preferred to remain anonymous.

Sending my draft manuscript out into the world was a particularly scary moment. A huge thank you goes to my beta-readers, Giles Bennett, Paul Breach, Helen Burgess, Ruth Davison, Camilla Faith, Maeve Hawker, David Murphy, Jane Olds, Kathryn Ryan, Ulrich Tennie and Louise Zekaria, for generously taking the time to read it, letting me know what you enjoyed most about it and not shying away from telling me what didn't work for you. Your thoughtful, perceptive comments were invaluable in helping me to improve *The Future of Time* for future readers. Thank you too to Ella Coleman at Mozarella graphic design for your skilful illustrations.

The next shout-out is for my many friends from home and work who have asked how it was going, encouraged me past my doubts, listened patiently when I've rambled on about the book and cheered my progress in person and online. You all rock! I can't list everyone here, but special thanks go to Cherry Aicardi-Brooker, Caroline Daly, Kristina Edwards, Nicola Finney, Lucy Ford, Gilly Marshall, Emma Omnet, Catherine Speed, Annabel Stonor, Sarah Tennant, Lisa Wheeler, and fellow authors Jo Richardson, Lucy Ryan, Alice Sheldon and Grace Marshall.

Finally, thank you to my wonderful family for always believing in me and being there for me, not just with this book but always. To my mother Judith Bennett, for all your love and encouragement from the very beginning. To my father Nicholas, so loved and missed. To Andrew Bennett and Giles Bennett for your sibling banter that livened up my long winter of writing. To June Beedham, for your cheerful chats, lunches and niece-hosting, which gave me welcome respites. To our fabulous 'big kids', Will and Becca, for your interest, entertaining opinions and enthusiasm all the way from Australia. To my dearest Isabella, budding writer and illustrator, who wrote and drew me so many messages of encouragement and pride over the past year and a half. I love you to the moon and stars and back.

Lastly, to my husband John, for the countless times you've listened to me rabbit on about this book, helped me think through the tricky bits, sent me links to read and let me pick your brain as an organization and leadership expert, and as a 'knower of random stuff'; for picking up the slack at home when I was lost in book world; and for your unswerving faith in my abilities.

Notes

Introduction

[1] Edgar Schein, *Organisational culture & leadership*, 4th ed., 2010.

[2] 'British workers putting in longest hours in the EU, TUC analysis finds', TUC, 17 April 2019, www.tuc.org.uk/news/british-workers-putting-longest-hours-eu-tuc-analysis-finds.

[3] 'Paying the price: The cost of mental health care in England to 2026', The King's Fund, 2008, www.kingsfund.org.uk/sites/default/files/Paying-the-Price-the-cost-of-mental-health-care-England-2026-McCrone-Dhanasiri-Patel-Knapp-Lawton-Smith-Kings-Fund-May-2008_0.pdf.

[4] 'Poor mental health costs UK employers up to £45 billion a year', Deloitte, 22 January 2020, www2.deloitte.com/uk/en/pages/press-releases/articles/poor-mental-health-costs-uk-employers-up-to-pound-45-billion-a-year.html.

Chapter 1: Time today

[1] For example, McKinsey, 'Why diversity matters', 2015, www.mckinsey.com/business-functions/organization/our-insights/why-diversity-matters#; Deloitte, *The diversity & inclusion revolution: 8 powerful truths*, 2018, www2.deloitte.com/content/dam/insights/us/articles/4209_Diversity-and-inclusion-revolution/DI_Diversity-and-inclusion-revolution.pdf;

BCG, 'How diverse leadership teams boost innovation', 2018, www.bcg.com/en-us/publications/2018/how-diverse-leadership-teams-boost-innovation.

[2] P. Drucker, *The effective executive: The definitive guide to getting the right things done*, HarperCollins, 2017.

[3] J. Kodz, S. Davis, D. Lain, M. Strebler, J. Rick, P. Bates, J. Cummings & N. Meager, *Working long hours: A review of the evidence*, Institute for Employment Studies, 2003, www.employment-studies.co.uk/resource/working-long-hours-review-evidence.

[4] Kodz et al., *Working long hours*.

[5] D. Kahneman, *Thinking fast and slow*, Penguin, 2012.

[6] D. Levitin, *The organized mind*, Penguin, 2015.

[7] D. Levitin, *The organized mind*.

[8] US Department of Defense (DoD) news briefing about the invasion of Iraq, 12 February 2002, https://youtu.be/GiPe1OiKQuk.

[9] D. Levitin, *The organized mind*.

[10] R.E. Baumeister, E. Bratslavsky, M. Muraven & D.M. Tice, *Ego depletion: Is the active self a limited resource?* Case Western Reserve University, 1998.

[11] TUC, 'Workers in the UK put in more than £32 billion worth of unpaid overtime last year – TUC analysis', 1 March 2019, www.tuc.org.uk/news/workers-uk-put-more-%C2%A332-billion-worth-unpaid-overtime-last-year-tuc-analysis. Based on ONS data from the Labour Force Survey (July–September 2018) and the Annual Survey of Hours and Earnings (2018).

[12] CIPD Good Work Index 2020, www.cipd.co.uk/Images/good-work-index-full-report-2020-2_tcm18-79210.pdf.

[13] TUC, 'Work Your Proper Hours Day – tackling the culture of unpaid overtime', www.tuc.org.uk/blogs/work-your-proper-hours-day-%E2%80%93-tackling-culture-unpaid-overtime.

[14] Working Families, https://workingfamilies.org.uk/gohomeontimeday.

[15] 'We just can't unplug: 2 in 5 employees only take up to half their annual leave', Glassdoor, 24 May 2018, www.glassdoor.co.uk/blog/we-just-cant-unplug-2-in-3-employees-report-working-while-on-vacation.

[16] The Workforce Institute at UKG, 'Physical safety, psychological security, job stability: Employees worldwide share top COVID-19 concerns for the workplace of today and tomorrow', www.kronos.com/about-us/newsroom/physical-safety-psychological-security-job-stability-employees-worldwide-share-top-covid-19-concerns.

[17] E. DeFilippis, S.M. Impink, M. Singell, J.T. Polzer & R. Sadun, *Collaborating during Coronavirus: The impact of COVID-19 on the nature of work*, National Bureau of Economic Research, July 2020, www.nber.org/papers/w27612.

[18] Health & Safety Executive reports on work-related stress, anxiety or depression statistics in Great Britain, 2020, www.hse.gov.uk/statistics/causdis/stress.pdf.

[19] The Professional Occupations and Associate Professional and Technical Occupations categories had statistically significantly higher rates of work-related stress, depression or anxiety than those for all occupations. For the three-year period averaged over 2017/18–2019/20, the Professional Occupations category had 2260 cases per 100,000 people employed and the Associate Professional and Technical Occupations category had 1880 cases per 100,000 people employed, compared with 1570 cases for all occupational groups.

[20] Rand Europe, 'The value of the sleep economy', www.rand.org/randeurope/research/projects/the-value-of-the-sleep-economy.html. Currency conversion based on exchange rates as at 12 July 2021.

[21] 'Parents now spend twice as much time with their children as they did 50 years ago', *The Economist*, 27 November 2017, www.economist.com/graphic-detail/2017/11/27/parents-now-spend-twice-as-much-time-with-their-children-as-50-years-ago?fsrc=scn%2Ftw%2Fte%2Fbl%2Fed%2F.

[22] E. Mamo, 'How to combat the rise of workplace loneliness', *Total Jobs*, 19 March 2020, www.totaljobs.com/advice/how-to-combat-the-rise-of-workplace-loneliness.

Chapter 2: Time blindness

[1] Statistia, 4 November 2020, www.statista.com/statistics/881202/recruitment-average-time-to-hire-by-industry-worldwide.

[2] LinkedIn Global Recruiting Trends, 1 December 2016, www.linkedin.com/pulse/global-recruiting-trends-2017-andrew-gagen.

[3] Working Families, https://workingfamilies.org.uk/campaigns/happy-to-talk-flexible-working.

[4] Conor D'Arcy & David Finch, *The great escape? Low pay and progression in the UK's labour market*, Social Mobility Commission, 2017, https://assets.

publishing.service.gov.uk/government/uploads/system/uploads/
attachment_data/file/652973/The_Great_Escape_-_Report.pdf.
[5] Timewise Flexible Jobs Index, 2020, https://timewise.co.uk/article/
flexible-jobs-index.

Chapter 3: Time defects

[1] 'In the boardroom, size matters', Board Intelligence and Cambridge Judge Institute, 9 March 2017, www.boardintelligence.com/blog/in-the-boardroom-size-matters.

[2] Financial Reporting Council, *2018 guidance on board effectiveness*, www.frc.org.uk/getattachment/61232f60-a338-471b-ba5a-bfed25219147/2018-Guidance-on-Board-Effectiveness-FINAL.PDF.

[3] R. Sengupta, 'Pandemic speeds up overhauls at law firms', *Financial Times*, 7 August 2020, www.ft.com/content/849a894c-bd1b-11ea-a05d-efc604854c3f.

[4] Time survey conducted by me in November 2020. Response to the question 'What are the biggest time "drains" for you at work?'.

[5] M. Goldsmith, 'Reducing negativity in the workplace', *Harvard Business Review*, 8 October 2007, https://hbr.org/2007/10/reducing-negativity-in-the-wor and RL#20; Peter Bregman, 'The next time you want to complain at work, do this instead', *Harvard Business Review*, 17 May 2018, https://hbr.org/2018/05/the-next-time-you-want-to-complain-at-work-do-this-instead.

[6] A. Andrew, S. Cattan, M. Costa Dias, C. Farquharson, L. Kraftman, S. Krutikova, A. Phimister & A. Sevilla, *Parents, especially mothers, paying heavy price for lockdown*, Institute for Fiscal Studies, 2020, www.ifs.org.uk/publications/14861.

[7] 'In search of lost time: Why is everyone so busy?', *The Economist*, 20 December 2014, www.economist.com/christmas-specials/2014/12/20/why-is-everyone-so-busy.

[8] Levitin, *The organized mind.*

[9] 'Long working hours increasing deaths from heart disease and stroke', World Health Organization & International Labour Organization, 17 May 2021, www.who.int/news/item/17-05-2021-long-working-hours-increasing-deaths-from-heart-disease-and-stroke-who-ilo.

[10] 'Employee happiness dropped dramatically during lockdown – Aviva research', CIPD, 10 December 2020, www.peoplemanagement.

co.uk/news/articles/employee-happiness-dropped-dramatically-during-lockdown.

[11] A.M. Richardsen & S.B. Matthiesen, 'Managers: Less stress when work relationships are good', BI Norwegian Business School, August 2014, www.sciencedaily.com/releases/2014/08/140812121737.htm.

[12] Time survey conducted by me in November 2020. In response to the question: 'How much time freedom do you feel you have during a typical working week?'.

[13] UK Government, *Race in the workplace: The McGregor-Smith review*, 28 February 2017, https://assets.publishing.service.gov.uk/government/uploads/system/uploads/attachment_data/file/594336/race-in-workplace-mcgregor-smith-review.pdf.

[14] A.J. Maule & B. Summers, 'Effects of time pressure on managerial decision-making', unpublished working paper, 2016, https://cdr.leeds.ac.uk/wp-content/uploads/sites/102/2017/10/time-pressure-working-paper.pdf.

[15] Z. Gorvett, 'Can you work yourself to death?', *BBC Worklife*, 13 September 2016, www.bbc.com/worklife/article/20160912-is-there-such-thing-as-death-from-overwork.

[16] M. Kivimäki et al., 'Long working hours and risk of coronary heart disease and stroke: A systematic review and meta-analysis of published and unpublished data for 603 838 individuals', *The Lancet*, 386(10005), 1739–46, www.thelancet.com/journals/lancet/article/PIIS0140-6736(15)60295-1/fulltext.

[17] Embracing the age of ambiguity: Re-invigorating the workforce in a rapidly evolving world. Aviva. November 2020. https://www.aviva.co.uk/adviser/documents/view/br01550c.pdf.

[18] Fertility Network UK, https://fertilitynetworkuk.org.

[19] BITC, *Race at work 2015*, 2015, https://www.bitc.org.uk/report/race-at-work-2015.

[20] BITC, *Race at work: Black voices*, 23 August 2020, www.bitc.org.uk/report/race-at-work-black-voices-report.

[21] Law Society, 'Race for inclusion: The experiences of Black, Asian and minority ethnic solicitors', December 2020, www.lawsociety.org.uk/topics/research/race-for-inclusion-the-experiences-of-black-asian-and-minority-ethnic-solicitors.

[22] BITC, *Race at work: Black voices*.

[23] Law Society, 'Race for inclusion'.

24 Law Society, 'Race for inclusion'.

25 Chartered Management Institute, *Management transformed: Managing in a marathon crisis,* 18 November 2020, https://issuu.com/cmi_/docs/management_transformed.

26 L. Worrall, C. Cooper, M. Kerrin, A. LaBand, A. Rosselli & P. Woodman, *The quality of working life: Exploring managers' wellbeing, motivation and productivity,* January 2016, www.managers.org.uk/~/media/Files/Quality%20of%20working%20life/Quality%20of%20Working%20Life%20-%20full%20report%20-%20January%202016.pdf.

27 BCG, 'It's frontline leaders who make or break progress on diversity', March 2020, www.bcg.com/publications/2020/frontline-leaders-make-break-progress-diversity?linkId=98703918.

Chapter 4: Changing times

1 ONS, 'Overview of the UK population: January 2021', www.ons.gov.uk/peoplepopulationandcommunity/populationandmigration/populationestimates/articles/overviewoftheukpopulation/january2021.

2 'Population and economic activities in the UK', *BBC Bitesize,* www.bbc.co.uk/bitesize/guides/zx3bwxs/revision/1.

3 Fertility Network UK, https://fertilitynetworkuk.org.

4 ONS, 'Families and households in the UK: 2019', www.ons.gov.uk/peoplepopulationandcommunity/birthsdeathsandmarriages/families/bulletins/familiesandhouseholds/2019#multi-family-households-are-the-fastest-growing-household-type-in-the-uk-but-currently-represent-the-smallest-share-of-households.

5 Working Families & Bright Horizons, *Modern Family Index 2019,* www.workingfamilies.org.uk/wp-content/uploads/2019/02/BH_MFI_Report_2019_Full-Report_Final.pdf.

6 *Good work: The Taylor review of modern working practices,* July 2017, https://assets.publishing.service.gov.uk/government/uploads/system/uploads/attachment_data/file/627671/good-work-taylor-review-modern-working-practices-rg.pdf.

7 *Good work: The Taylor review of modern working practices.*

8 CIPD, *To gig or not to gig? Stories from the modern economy,* 17 March 2017, www.cipd.co.uk/knowledge/work/trends/gig-economy-report.

9 Companies register activities: 2020 to 2021, Companies House, 24 June 2021, www.gov.uk/government/statistics/companies-register-activities-

statistical-release-2020-to-2021/companies-register-activities-2020-to-2021.

[10] Deloitte, 'Rewriting the rules for the digital age: 2017 global human capital trends', www2.deloitte.com/us/en/insights/multimedia/infographics/human-capital-trends.html.

[11] UK Government, *Race in the workplace*.

[12] McKinsey, *Why diversity matters*, 1 January 2015, www.mckinsey.com/business-functions/organization/our-insights/why-diversity-matters.

[13] UK Government, *Race in the workplace*.

[14] Willis Towers Watson & Bloomberg, 'Companies with greater gender diversity in leadership roles create a more positive experience for all employees', 23 September 2020, www.willistowerswatson.com/en-US/News/2020/09/companies-with-greater-gender-diversity-in-leadership-roles-create-a-more-positive-experience.

[15] CIPD, *To gig or not to gig?*

[16] S. Farazi, S. Jones & K. Savage, 'How has COVID impacted women in the workplace?' People Management, 18 January 2021, www.peoplemanagement.co.uk/voices/comment/how-has-covid-impacted-women-in-the-workplace.

[17] CEHR, 'How coronavirus has affected equality and human rights', 20 October 2020, www.equalityhumanrights.com/en/publication-download/how-coronavirus-has-affected-equality-and-human-rights.

[18] CMI, *Management transformed: Managing in a marathon crisis*.

[19] J. Bersin, *Business resilience: The global COVID-19 pandemic response study*, 2020, https://ss-usa.s3.amazonaws.com/c/308463326/media/16635f853453eec9687518946851882/covid%20research%20report%20v5.pdf.

[20] Timewise Flexible Jobs Index 2020, https://timewise.co.uk/article/flexible-jobs-index.

[21] Survey by Cityparents of 481 professionals working in corporate roles, September–October 2020, www.cityparents.co.uk/SiteAssets/Files/Cityparents%20Survey%20Report%202020.pdf.

[22] '6 ways our work habits will change in 2021', 13 January 2021, www.helenbeedham.com/article-6-ways-our-work-habits-will-change-in-2021.

[23] R. Sengupta, 'Pandemic speeds up overhaul at law firms, *Financial Times*, 7 August 2020, www.ft.com/content/849a894c-bd1b-11ea-a05d-efc604854c3f.

[24] *WEF Future of Jobs Report 2020*, 20 October 2020, www.weforum. org/reports/the-future-of-jobs-report-2020#report-nav.

[25] J. Spataro, '2 years of digital transformation in 2 months', Microsoft, 30 April 2020, www.microsoft.com/en-us/microsoft-365/ blog/2020/04/30/2-years-digital-transformation-2-months.

[26] World Economic Forum, *The future of jobs report 2020*, www.weforum. org/reports/the-future-of-jobs-report-2020#report-nav.

[27] McKinsey & Co, 'From thinking about the next normal to making it work: What to stop, start, and accelerate', May 2020, www. mckinsey.com/featured-insights/leadership/from-thinking-about- the-next-normal-to-making-it-work-what-to-stop-start-and-accelerate#.

[28] PwC, *Digital transformation in financial services*, YouTube, https://youtu. be/Gm0xwlzLECU.

[29] World Economic Forum, 'Professional services: Approaching a digital tipping point', https://reports.weforum.org/digital-transformation/ professional-services-approaching-a-digital-tipping-point.

[30] World Economic Forum, *The future of jobs report 2020*.

[31] B. Schulte, *Overwhelmed: Work, love and play when no one has the time*, Farrar, Straus and Giroux, 2014.

[32] Worrall et al., *The quality of working life*.

[33] Research by the charity Relate, www.stylist.co.uk/life/lunch-for- one-again-work-loneliness-workplace-friendships-study-colleagues- happiness-health/65399209.

[34] 'It's time to acknowledge CEO loneliness', *Harvard Business Review*, 15 February 2012, https://hbr.org/2012/02/its-time-to-acknowledge- ceo-lo.

[35] Arabesque Partners & University of Oxford, *From the stockholder to the stakeholder: How sustainability can drive financial outperformance*, March 2015, https://arabesque.com/research/From_the_stockholder_to_the_ stakeholder_web.pdf.

[36] www.globalreporting.org.

[37] G. Kell, 'The remarkable rise of ESG', *Forbes*, 11 July 2018, www. forbes.com/sites/georgkell/2018/07/11/the-remarkable-rise-of-esg.

[38] A. Francke OBE, 'The new formula for corporate reputation', CMI, 15 September 2020, www.managers.org.uk/knowledge-and-insights/ article/the-new-formula-for-corporate-reputation.

[39] 'Rio Tinto CEO quits after backlash over Aboriginal site destruction', *Financial Times*, 11 September 2020, www.ft.com/content/ dd75d6da-f047-49d4-9b2e-cfc2ef95df00.

[40] McKinsey & Co., 'Diversity wins: How inclusion matters', 19 May 2020, www.mckinsey.com/featured-insights/diversity-and-inclusion/diversity-wins-how-inclusion-matters#.

[41] Carol Morrison, 'Don't let the shift to remote work sabotage your inclusion initiatives', Ic4p.com, 31 March 2020, www.i4cp.com/coronavirus/dont-let-the-shift-to-remote-work-sabotage-your-inclusion-initiatives.

[42] Our CEO's response to the latest Social Mobility Commission Report, Social Mobility Foundation, 10 June 2020, www.socialmobility.org.uk/2020/06/our-ceos-response-to-the-latest-social-mobility-commission-report-10-june-2020.

[43] IES, 'Labour market statistics', November 2020, www.employment-studies.co.uk/resource/labour-market-statistics-november-2020; RL#174, 'The impacts of the coronavirus crisis on the labour market. IES', December 2020, www.employment-studies.co.uk/resource/impacts-coronavirus-crisis-labour-market.

[44] Russell Reynolds, 'The time is now: How companies and leaders can join the fight for racial justice', 8 July 2020, www.russellreynolds.com/insights/thought-leadership/time-is-now-how-companies-leaders-can-join-fight-for-racial-justice.

[45] Green Park, 'Britain's top firms failing black leaders | Green Park's annual business leaders index records no black chairs, CEOs or CFOs at FTSE 100 companies', 3 February 2021, www.green-park.co.uk/news/britain-s-top-firms-failing-black-leaders-green-park-s-annual-business-leaders-index-records-no-black-chairs-ceos-or-cfos-at-ftse-100-companies/s228922.

[46] Ethnicity pay gap reporting consultation, 11 October 2018 to 11 January 2019, www.gov.uk/government/consultations/ethnicity-pay-reporting.

[47] Stonewall, *LGBT in Britain – work report*, 25 April 2015, www.stonewall.org.uk/power-inclusive-workplaces.

[48] 'Transgender hate crimes recorded by police go up 81%', *BBC News*, 27 June 2019, www.bbc.co.uk/news/uk-48756370.

[49] 'Moody's says Lloyds' ethnic diversity plan is "credit positive"', *Financial Times*, 24 July 2020, www.ft.com/content/f577f05f-e943-482a-841c-a85c71bf306a.

[50] 'Reporting on the new Corporate Governance Code is a mixed picture', Financial Reporting Council, 26 November 2020, www.frc.org.uk/news/november-2020/reporting-on-the-new-corporate-governance-code-is.

[51] ICO, *Guide to the UK General Data Protection Regulation (UK GDPR)*, https://ico.org.uk/for-organizations/guide-to-data-protection/guide-to-the-general-data-protection-regulation-gdpr.

[52] UK Government, 'Government to protect workers' rights and clamp down on workplace abuse with powerful new body', 8 June 2021, www.gov.uk/government/news/government-to-protect-workers-rights-and-clamp-down-on-workplace-abuse-with-powerful-new-body.

[53] UK Government, 'Understanding off-payroll working (IR35)', March 2020, www.gov.uk/guidance/understanding-off-payroll-working-ir35.

[54] Financial Conduct Authority, 'Senior Managers and Certification Regime: Solo-regulated firms', March 2017, www.fca.org.uk/firms/senior-managers-certification-regime/solo-regulated-firms.

[55] 'Kwarteng confirms government review of UK employment law', *Financial Times*, 19 January 2021, www.ft.com/content/ab8d876c-bc65-441e-8b04-051d3be124c9.

Chapter 5: Out of time

[1] John Maynard Keynes, 'Economic possibilities for our grandchildren' in *Essays in persuasion*, Harcourt Brace, 1930, www.econ.yale.edu/smith/econ116a/keynes1.pdf.

[2] Emma Luxton, 'Does working fewer hours make you more productive?', World Economic Forum, 4 March 2016, www.weforum.org/agenda/2016/03/does-working-fewer-hours-make-you-more-productive.

[3] Nicholas Crafts & Terence C. Mills, 'UK productivity slowdown unprecedented in 250 years – new study shows', Universities of Sussex & Loughborough, 12 February 2020, www.sussex.ac.uk/business-school/internal/newsandevents/placementawards?page=13&id=51253.

[4] J. Kodz, S. Davis, D. Lain, M. Strebler, J. Rick, P. Bates, J. Cummings & N. Meager, *Working long hours: A review of the evidence*, Institute for Employment Studies, October 2003, www.employment-studies.co.uk/resource/working-long-hours-review-evidence.

[5] Worrall et al., *The quality of working life*.

[6] A. Whillans, *Time Smart*, Harvard Business Review Press, 2020.

[7] B. Jensen, *Simplicity: The new competitive advantage in a world of more, better, faster*, http://showcase.netins.net/web/jjjensen/books/book05_Simplicity.html.

[8] World Economic Forum, *The future of jobs report 2020*.

[9] European Commission, 'The gender pay gap situation in the EU', 2019, https://ec.europa.eu/info/policies/justice-and-fundamental-rights/gender-equality/equal-pay/gender-pay-gap-situation-eu_en.

[10] Office for National Statistics, 'Gender pay gap in the UK: 2020', 3 November 2020, www.ons.gov.uk/employmentandlabourmarket/peopleinwork/earningsandworkinghours/bulletins/genderpaygapintheuk/2020.

[11] Bloomberg, 'Understanding the emotional tax on black professionals in the workplace', 3 February 2021, www.bloomberg.com/company/stories/understanding-the-emotional-tax-on-black-professionals-in-the-workplace.

[12] D. Kahneman, *Thinking fast and slow*.

[13] US Department of Defense (DoD) news briefing about the invasion of Iraq, 12 February 2002, https://youtu.be/GiPe1OiKQuk.

[14] 'Engage for Success: Nailing the evidence', https://engageforsuccess.org/nailing-the-evidence.

[15] Engage for Success, 'What is employee engagement?', https://engageforsuccess.org/what-is-employee-engagement.

[16] Economies ranked by GDP. Source: Kenexa 2009 via Engage for Success website, https://engageforsuccess.org.

[17] 'Trainee retention', *Chambers Student News*, March 2019, www.chambersstudent.co.uk/where-to-start/newsletter/trainee-retention.

[18] Law Society, 'Race for inclusion'.

[19] 'How consulting leaders can tackle the retention problem of juniors', *Consultancy News*, 4 December 2018, www.consultancy.uk/news/19569/how-consulting-leaders-can-tackle-the-retention-problem-of-juniors.

[20] 'Financial services employees are surprisingly happy, except in the Middle East', *E-Financial News*, 16 June 2014, www.efinancialcareers.co.uk/news/2014/06/financial-services-employees-happier-think-except-middle-east.

[21] A. Isham, S. Mair & T. Jackson, 'Wellbeing and productivity: A review of the literature', University of Bradford, January 2020, https://bradscholars.brad.ac.uk/bitstream/handle/10454/18268/pp-wellbeing-report.pdf?sequence=2.

[22] 'When bankers burn out: Sifting through the ashes', *E-financial Careers*, 17 June 2014, www.efinancialcareers.co.uk/news/2014/06/banker-burnout.

[23] 'Asana Anatomy of Work Index 2021: Work about work is dominating in a distributed world', *Business Wire*, 14 January 2021, www.businesswire.

com/news/home/20210114005374/en/Asana-Anatomy-of-Work-Index-2021-Work-About-Work-Is-Dominating-in-a-Distributed-World.

[24] Sarah Waters, 'Suicidal work: Work-related suicides are uncounted', *Hazards Magazine*, March 2017, www.hazards.org/suicide/suicidalwork.htm.

[25] 'Work-related stress, anxiety or depression statistics in Great Britain, 2020', *Health & Safety Executive*, 4 November 2020, www.hse.gov.uk/statistics/causdis/stress.pdf.

[26] UK Government, *Thriving at work: The Stevenson/Farmer review of mental health and employers*, 2017, https://assets.publishing.service.gov.uk/government/uploads/system/uploads/attachment_data/file/658145/thriving-at-work-stevenson-farmer-review.pdf.

[27] 'Mental health services are failing to meet rising demand, new TUC report reveals', TUC, 22 October 2018, www.tuc.org.uk/news/mental-health-services-are-failing-meet-rising-demand-new-tuc-report-reveals.

[28] T.C. Russ, E. Stamatakis, M. Hamer & M. Kivimäki, 'Association between psychological distress and mortality: Individual participant pooled analysis of 10 prospective cohort studies', *BMJ*, 345, www.bmj.com/content/345/bmj.e4933.

[29] *Good work: The Taylor review of modern working practices.*

[30] Quote drawn from *Good work: The Taylor review of modern working practices.*

[31] McKinsey, 'From thinking about the next normal to making it work: What to stop, start, and accelerate', May 2020, www.mckinsey.com/featured-insights/leadership/from-thinking-about-the-next-normal-to-making-it-work-what-to-stop-start-and-accelerate#.

Chapter 6: Time reimagined

[1] 'In search of lost time: Why is everyone so busy?', *The Economist*, 20 December 2014, www.economist.com/christmas-specials/2014/12/20/why-is-everyone-so-busy.

[2] B. Gates & W. Buffet, *The power of questions*, with Charlie Rose. https://charlierose.com/videos/29774. 27 January 2017.

[3] D. Levitin, *The organized mind.*

[4] C. Newport, *Deep work: Rules for focused success in a distracted world*, Grand Central Publishing.

[5] UK Commission for Employment & Skills, *The future of work: Jobs and skills*, https://assets.publishing.service.gov.uk/government/uploads/system/uploads/attachment_data/file/303340/the_future_of_work_slide_pack.pdf.

[6] #10000BlackInterns, www.10000blackinterns.com.

[7] F. Brooks Taplett, J. Garcia-Alonso, M. Krentz & Mai-Britt Poulsen, 'It's frontline leaders who make or break progress on diversity', BCG, March 2020, www.bcg.com/publications/2020/frontline-leaders-make-break-progress-diversity?linkId=98703918.

[8] Worrall et al., *The quality of working life*.

[9] Richardsen & Matthiesen, 'Managers: Less stress when work relationships are good'.

[10] George Orwell, *Animal farm*, Secker and Warburg, 1945.

[11] D. Kahneman, *Thinking fast and slow*.

[12] J. Suzman, 'The 300,000-year case for the 15-hour week', *Financial Times*, October 2020, www.ft.com/content/8dd71dc3-4566-48e0-a1d9-3e8bd2b3f60f.

[13] *Good work: The Taylor review of modern working practices*.

[14] Worrall et al., *The quality of working life*.

[15] P.M. Senge, 'The leader's new work: Building learning organizations', *Sloan Management Review*, 32(1), 1990, https://sloanreview.mit.edu/article/the-leaders-new-work-building-learning-organizations.

[16] M. Heffernan, *Wilful blindness: Why we ignore the obvious at our peril*, Simon & Schuster, 2011.

Chapter 7: Time solutions

[1] 'Reporting on the new Corporate Governance Code is a mixed picture', FRC media release, 26 November 2020, www.frc.org.uk/news/november-2020/reporting-on-the-new-corporate-governance-code-is.

[2] D. Barton, J. Manyika, T. Koller, R. Palter, J. Godsall & J. Zoffer, 'Where companies with a long-term view outperform their peers', McKinsey & Co, 8 February 2017, www.mckinsey.com/featured-insights/long-term-capitalism/where-companies-with-a-long-term-view-outperform-their-peers.

[3] Brian Dive, 'Getting rid of grades to boost performance', *Strategy+Business*, 14 April 2009, www.strategy-business.com/article/li00120.

[4] David Wilkinson, 'How our emotions influence work groups and organizations – new research', *Oxford Review*, www.oxford-review.com/emotions-influence-groups.

[5] Requisite Organization International Institute, www.requisite.org/about.

[6] A Gallup study (2006) looking at data from over 23,000 business units has demonstrated that those with the highest engagement scores (top 25%) averaged 18% higher productivity than those with the lowest engagement scores (bottom 25%). Engage for Success, https://engageforsuccess.org/nailing-the-evidence.

[7] 'Reimagining how we work at Novartis', 15 October 2020, www.linkedin.com/pulse/reimagining-how-we-work-novartis-steven-baert/?trackingId=B%2BGnkmuZSsISfwHW8XezsQ%3D%3D.

[8] R. Calvert Jump & Will Stronge, 'The day after tomorrow: Stress tests, affordability and the roadmap to the four day week', *Autonomy*, 29 December 2020, https://autonomy.work/portfolio/dat.

[9] A. S-K. Pang, *Shorter*, Penguin, 2020.

[10] 'PwC says start when you like, leave when you like', *BBC News*, 31 March 2021, www.bbc.co.uk/news/business-56591189.

[11] 'Fascinating email facts', *Livewire*, 15 March 2020, www.lifewire.com/how-many-emails-are-sent-every-day-1171210.

[12] D.-E. Dubé, 'This is how much time you spend on work emails every day, according to a Canadian survey', *Global News*, 17 April 2017, https://globalnews.ca/news/3395457/this-is-how-much-time-you-spend-on-work-emails-every-day-according-to-a-canadian-survey.

[13] https://mindfulbusinesscharter.com.

[14] CMI, *Management transformed: Managing in a marathon crisis*.

[15] John Kotter, *A sense of urgency*, Harvard Business Press, 1 August 2008, www.kotterinc.com/book/a-sense-of-urgency.

[16] S. Denning, 'What is Agile?' *Forbes*, 13 August 2016, www.forbes.com/sites/stevedenning/2016/08/13/what-is-agile.

[17] Time survey conducted by me in November 2020. In response to the question, 'How many hours do you get each week for deep thinking/productive work, on average? Does this feel sufficient to do your best work?'

[18] Responses to time survey conducted by me in November 2020.

Chapter 8: Time and talent

[1] World Economic Forum, *Future of Jobs Report 2020*, 20 October 2020, www.weforum.org/reports/the-future-of-jobs-report-2020#report-nav.

[2] https://commonslibrary.parliament.uk/uber-at-the-supreme-court-who-is-a-worker.

[3] 'Goldman Sachs boss says "go extra mile" despite 95-hour week', *BBC News*, 24 March 2020, www.bbc.co.uk/news/business-56495463.

[4] 'Labour of love or love vs labour?', *Relate*, October 2016, www.relate.org.uk/policy-campaigns/our-campaigns/way-we-are-now-2016/work.

[5] Across six studies with 4,690 respondents. L.M. Giurge & A.V. Whillans, *Beyond material poverty: Why time poverty matters for individuals, organizations, and nations*, Harvard Business School, 1920, www.hbs.edu/faculty/Publication%20Files/20-051_9ccace07-ec9b-409e-a6aa-723f091422fb.pdf.

[6] 'Rise of the work less workforce', *Timewise*, February 2018, https://timewise.co.uk/article/press-release-rise-work-less-workforce/?type=article&loadMore=1&pageId=2&postsPerPage=8&order=menu_order&orderdir=DESC&category%5B0%5D=17&topic=-1&contenttype=-1&taxonomy=articlecategory&excludeId=-1&publicOnly=1&fromKH=0.

[7] https://workingfamilies.org.uk/employers/httfw.

[8] The Behavioural Insights Team & Friends Provident, *The behavioural economy*, 26 November 2020, www.bi.team/publications/the-behavioural-economy.

[9] 'Zurich sees leap in women applying for senior roles after offering all jobs as flexible', 17 November 2020, www.zurich.co.uk/en/about-us/media-centre/company-news/2020/zurich-sees-leap-in-women-applying-for-senior-roles-after-offering-all-jobs-as-flexible.

[10] 'What does work mean to us?', *Financial Times*, 7 October 2020 https://on.ft.com/3ntsdPU.

[11] Willis Towers Watson, *Flexible Work and Rewards Survey: 2021 Design and budget priorities*, www.willistowerswatson.com/en-US/News/2020/11/uptick-in-flexible-work-arrangements-leads-companies-to-consider-new-pay-models?utm_source=linkedin&utm_medium=social&utm_campaign=Modernizing-Total-Rewards_&utm_content=human+capital+and+benefits_5dc00c74-869d-480f-813c-b1d83692fa6e_&utm_term=.

[12] 'Hurrah for the companies giving employees more time off', *Financial Times*, 25 October 2020, www.ft.com/content/09a8fd2b-7630-4655-a892-ec045e1ca8a7.

[13] 'Goldman Sachs boss says "go extra mile"'.

[14] 'It's frontline leaders who make or break progress on diversity', BCG, 5 March 2020, www.bcg.com/publications/2020/frontline-leaders-make-break-progress-diversity?linkId=98703918.

[15] 'How consulting leaders can tackle the retention problem of juniors', *Consultancy News*, www.consultancy.uk/news/19569/how-consulting-leaders-can-tackle-the-retention-problem-of-juniors.

[16] *Good work: The Taylor review of modern working practices.*

[17] M. Nixon, *Pariahs: Hubris, reputation and organizational crises*, Libri, 2016.

[18] UK Government, *Race in the workplace.*

[19] Law Society, 'Race for inclusion'.

[20] 'Lack of face-to-face learning and networking could damage careers', *Personnel Today*, 16 October 2020, www.personneltoday.com/hr/lack-of-face-to-face-learning-and-networking-could-damage-careers.

[21] Pang, *Shorter.*

[22] Public Health England & Leeds Beckett University, *Interventions to prevent burnout in high risk individuals: Evidence review*, February 2016, https://assets.publishing.service.gov.uk/government/uploads/system/uploads/attachment_data/file/506777/25022016_Burnout_Rapid_Review_2015709.pdf.

[23] BITC Research, *The race at work black voices report*, 23 August 2020, www.bitc.org.uk/report/race-at-work-black-voices-report.

[24] Bloomberg, 'Understanding the emotional tax on black professionals in the workplace', 3 February 2021, www.bloomberg.com/company/stories/understanding-the-emotional-tax-on-black-professionals-in-the-workplace.

[25] Stonewall, *LGBT in Britain: Work report*, 25 April 2018, www.stonewall.org.uk/power-inclusive-workplaces.

[26] www.fertifa.com/employers.

[27] 'Companies mine employee networks for growth', *Financial Times*, 18 November 2020, www.ft.com/content/65de3385-3c76-4171-88ab-42388bda2dac?shareType=nongift.

[28] CMI, *Management transformed: Managing in a marathon crisis.*

[29] 'Innovative Lawyers Europe: Constant updates of roles', *Financial Times*, 2 October 2020, www.ft.com/content/f9360ade-8d3f-498d-850a-b44a1d07a3a2.

[30] 'Countering the tyranny of the clock', *The Economist*, 17 October 2020, www.economist.com/business/2020/10/17/countering-the-tyranny-of-the-clock.

Chapter 9: Ahead of time

[1] Sources: Helen Beedham's call with Anette Bohm on 16 April 2021; KBC Group annual report 2020 www.kbc.com/content/dam/kbccom/doc/investor-relations/Results/jvs-2020/jvs-2020-grp-en.pdf?zone=footer-2; KBC press release 26 October 2018, www.kbc.com/content/dam/kbccom/doc/20181026_PB_TeamBlue4_ENG.pdf.

[2] Sources: Helen Beedham's call with David Henderson, Chief Human Resources Officer, on 13 April 2021; David Henderson's talk at Willis Towers Watson Total Rewards Conference, 24 February 2021; Zurich annual report 2020–21, www.zurich.com/en/annual-report/2020; Zurich Innovation Championship, www.zurich.com/en/campaigns/zic.

Chapter 10: Taking stock of time

[1] Perceived Stress Scale, available from Mind Garden, www.mindgarden.com; W. Schaufeli & A. Bakker, *Utrecht Work Engagement Scale*, 2003, www.wilmarschaufeli.nl/publications/Schaufeli/Test%20Manuals/Test_manual_UWES_English.pdf; Oldenburgh Burnout Inventory: see E. Demerouti, A.B. Bakker, I. Vardakou & A. Kantas, 'The convergent validity of two burnout instruments: A multitrait-multimethod analysis', *European Journal of Psychological Assessment*, 19(1), 2003, 12–23.

[2] E.H. Schein, *Organizational culture and leadership*, 4th ed., Jossey-Bass, 2010.

[3] R. Beckhard & R. Harris, *Organizational transitions: Managing complex change*, Addison-Wesley, 1987.

Chapter 11: Time strategies

[1] G. Gupta, J. Kotter & V. Ahktar, *Change: How Organizations Achieve Hard-to-Imagine Results In Uncertain and Volatile Times*, Wiley, 2021.

[2] Worrall et al., *The quality of working life*.

Chapter 12: Time after time

[1] 'Amateur manager' as described by John Board, 'Mission critical: The hot topics', CMI, 15 December 2020, www.managers.org.uk/knowledge-and-insights/article/mission-critical-the-management-hot-topics.

[2] The Growth Mindset Institute, www.growthmindsetinstitute.org.

[3] Growth Mindset Institute, 'Growth mindset and the future of work', 5 February 2020, www.growthmindsetinstitute.org/2020/02/05/growth-mindset-and-the-future-of-work.

[4] The Good Business Charter, www.goodbusinesscharter.com.

[5] www.4dayweek.co.uk.

[6] https://bcorporation.uk.

[7] https://betterbusinessact.org.

Appendix 4: Toolkit for re-working time

[1] B.W. Tuckman, 'Developmental sequence in small groups', *Psychological Bulletin*, 63(6), 1965, 384–99.

[2] S.R. Covey, *First things first*, Simon & Schuster, 2003.

[3] M. Pedler, *Action learning for managers*, Routledge, 2008.

Index

Note: Page numbers followed by the letter n indicate end-of-chapter notes, e.g. 19n19 refers to note 19 on page 19. Page numbers in *italics* refer to figures.